SPOONERISMS, SYCOPHANTS, AND SOPS

Spoonerisms, Sycophants, and Sops

DONALD CHAIN BLACK

1817

HARPER & ROW, PUBLISHERS, New York
Cambridge, Philadelphia, San Francisco, Washington
London, Mexico City, São Paulo, Singapore, Sydney

As both peruser and purveyor of etymologies, I have owed much to the compendious lexical works of Wilfred Funk, Willard Espy, and Eric Partridge. Dozens of little gem books like those of Rosie Boycott, John Train, and Philip Howard have been of great value, too. To assemble this book I have listened to the language and read the words of hundreds of speakers and writers, endeavoring in each case to identify the source.

I gratefully acknowledge Paris Junior College's Division of Continuing Education, through which I taught the series of courses that led to the writing of this book.

Grateful acknowledgment is made for permission to reprint:

From *Journal of the American Medical Association* 249(17):2304–2305, May 6, 1983. Copyright 1983, American Medical Association.

From *Journal of the American Medical Association* 237(7):677, February 14, 1977. Copyright 1977, American Medical Association.

FIRST EDITION

Designed by Sidney Feinberg

Library of Congress Cataloging-in-Publication Data

Black, Donald Chain.
  Spoonerisms, sycophants, and sops.

  Includes index.
  1. English language—Etymology.   I. Title.
PE1574.B57   1988   422   87-45832
ISBN 0-06-015886-7

88 89 90 91 92 HC 10 9 8 7 6 5 4 3 2 1

For Virginia

.

Preface

Some years ago the distinguished poet and dramatist W. H. Auden came to a northeastern college in the United States. Hired for one year as poet-in-residence and lecturer, he had agreed to teach a single poetry course as well. To encourage student participation he asked that the class enrollment be limited to twenty. Auden and his work were popular then as now, and two hundred students signed up for the course.

When members of the English department offered their help in winnowing the applicants, the poet thanked them but said he'd do it himself. With only a secretary to help, he interviewed all the students who had applied. The job proved to be a long one, but by the end of the day Auden had selected his twenty class members.

Several days later a curious department chairman asked him what criteria he had used to make his selections, and Auden said he had used just one: he had spoken to each applicant in an informal sort of way, he said, until he saw some evidence that the student *loved words*. About one out of ten had seemed to possess that particular trait, so that the class was filled to his satisfaction.

Why do people love words? Probably for pretty much the same mysterious reasons that people love each other: an endless set of motivations as curious and complex as the personality itself. Some word lovers are interested in the origins and histories of words, and others are intrigued by relationships among words. Still others search for little-known facts about words, facts which bring words and language to life. That a *kangaroo* is etymologically the same thing as a *nitwit* is a tidbit of linguistic minutia that will be relished by any dedicated logophile. The lover of words who fondly remembers the Reverend W. A. Spooner (who once preached upon "Kinquering Congs" and gave us forever his name for any such humorous inversion) will be intrigued as well as dismayed to learn that the father of the spoonerism suffered from a brain dysfunction considerably more extensive than professorial absentmindedness. The wordmonger who has gleefully watched *egregious* slide from its former lofty and distinguished meaning to its present position of shame is only a little less delighted to see *jazz* (once synonymous with that most obscene of all words) "cleaned up" in an even shorter historical period.

That the reasons for relishing these—and almost a thousand other word origins presented in this book—remain ineffable only heightens etymological curiosity. Try your hand at the questions that fill the pages of this book and journey into the fascinating world of words.

SPOONERISMS, SYCOPHANTS, AND SOPS

Mark the one word in the list that does not go with all the other words:

tromp
blackmail
slithy
chastigate
chortle

Each of these words save one is a portmanteau word. Lewis Carroll used this term (from the type of large suitcase that opens into two hinged compartments) to describe a single word made by amalgamating two others. "Well, *slithy* means 'lithe and slimy,'" Humpty Dumpty says to Alice, ". . . You see it's like a portmanteau—there are two meanings packed up into one word."

Frumious (fuming + furious) and *chortle (chuckle + snort)* and *mimsy (miserable + flimsy)* are Carroll's very own, and his *galumph (gallop + triumph)* is ever so much more adroit than the popular *tromp (tramp + stomp)*.

Portmanteau words are coined every day of this compacted world, some of them more precise and some more colorful than their components. My banker brother is sometimes sterner than scolding but less than harsh with an errant employee when he finds it necessary to *chastigate (chastise + castigate)* him; his original* verb describes exactly what he means. And my sister-in-law unconsciously but vividly described a fellow teacher's flight from the schoolyard upon hearing some alarming news, saying, "She took to her heels in a *frantic.*" *(frenzy + panic)* Never send two words when one will do, particularly if it's more colorful anyway.

Good portmanteau words are a form of neologism and like the neologism require no explanation, yet possess their own flavor and specificity. The neologism *socialite* enjoyed instant recognition and use when it was coined by a *Time* magazine writer in 1929, but the portmanteau word *beautility (beauty + utility)* seems destined for a short life. After Carroll's, my favorite in this category has to be *Noxzema (knocks + eczema)* or maybe the neologism *monokini* (you can guess what *that* garment is).

Though it's likely that the *mail* in *blackmail* comes from the Middle English *maille*, "tribute," its probably spurious etymology is more colorful: an apocryphal story has it that *blackmail* is a word from chivalric times, when a penurious knight with no money for a squire to polish his armor would paint it black to keep away the rust. In those days, the loser at jousting by custom forfeited his horse and armor to the victor, who usually sold it back to the vanquished one, thereby making a verb from the name of the outfit he wore.

---

*Original and, most interestingly, unwitting.

All these words but one are contributions from one language and one book. Mark the eccentric word:

abishag
Shunammitism
slalom
shibboleth
leviathan

Robert Frost liked *abishag,* reading the sonorous name in his raspy old voice with relish:

> The witch that came (the withered hag)
> To wash the steps with pail and rag,
> Was once the beauty Abishag.

But unless you're fond of quoting Frost, this Hebrew word meaning "the mother's error"—for the child of a woman and a married man not her husband—might be difficult to work into polite conversation. Abishag was also the name of the young Shunammite virgin who was put into the bed of the aged and dying King David in an effort to rejuvenate him. This practice of *Shunammitism* described in the first chapter of I Kings turned out to be, alas, an ineffective remedy for senescence.

Knowing that their enemies could not pronounce the sound *sh-,* the biblical Gileadites used a test word to identify the fleeing Ephraimites. They chose *shibboleth,* a Hebrew word meaning "freshet," and this word has subsequently been broadened to mean any test word, catchphrase, or peculiarity of behavior that distinguishes the members of a group.

Though biblical scholars think that the monstrous sea creature that Job described was a crocodile, *leviathan* is now ap-

plied to anything unusually large for its kind, from Moby Dick
to a nuclear submarine.

Of course *slalom* is the only non-Hebrew, non–Old Testa-
ment word on the list. A Norwegian term for a downhill ski
race over a zigzag course, it is but a single letter different from
the Hebrew salutation invoking peace: *Shalom!*

W̲hat do these words have in common?

  trompe l'oeil
  quay
  argot
  charivari
  ghoti

My eleven-year-old son was charmed by his first trip to a
trompe l'oeil art exhibit. When we got home, I wrote down the
phrase to show him its meaning, and he commented, "Gee,
Dad, even the words fool your eye." His description fits all five
words on the list (French, from *tromper,* to deceive + *oeil,* eye:
trŏp-LÖY). "It really doesn't make any difference what the
French *do,*" Henry Higgins observes, "it's how they *say* it."

What do the words on this list have in common?

  new
  knit
  wail
  towed
  links
  bore
  might

As this homonymic list of animal names shows, Henry Higgins was right.

The British can be just as deceptive as the French, as in their word for "wharf," *quay* (kē), and their vowel-extravagant *queue* (kyo͞o). Pronouncing *argot* ignores the *-t.* The word for "a noisy mock serenade to a newly-wed couple," *shivaree* (shĭv′-ə-rē′), neither looks nor sounds like its Greek origin (*karēbaria,* heavy head), presumably the consequence of such revelry.

The *ghoti* story is a little like yesterday's fish, but I had to include it anyway, just because it's Shaw's. Surely Bernard Shaw has brought to linguistics more whimsical observations than any other writer. *Ghoti* is how one spells "fish," he japed: *gh* as in *enough, o* as in *women,* and *ti* as in *nation.*

Which word is out of place in the list below?

billets-doux
missives
epistles
chitties
belles-lettres

My students are awed at the vast amount of French that has "crept into the language," until they are reminded that French was the official language of England from 1066 to 1362. Three hundred years should leave some mementos, and love letters or *billets-doux* (*billet,* little note + *doux,* sweet) were at least as important in Europe as in England. We too have helped ourselves to the Latin *dulcis,* "sweet": *dulciana,* an organ stop with a sweet, thin note like a reed; *dulcet,* one stop above dulciana, pleasing to the ear, sweet to the taste; *dulcify,* to make sweet or agreeable; *dulcimer,* an instrument with wire strings over a sound box.

A *missive* is just a plain letter or message, while *epistle* shades the meaning to a more formal letter, like Paul wrote to the Romans and the Thessalonians. There is nothing formal about *chitties,* adapted by the British in India from the Hindi word for letter *(chitthi).* Just half of that word made it to America, where a chit is now only a bar bill or sometimes an IOU, as one might give for a gambling debt.

A literal translation of *belles-lettres* produces "fine letters," but the term actually describes a sort of literature written for its aesthetic value more than for edification or documentation. Once again the French language has deceived the eye.

Mark the one word on the list that's different from all the other words:

time
laced
stink
diaper
desserts
redivider

Jocular philologists maintain that the very first sentence ever spoken upon this earth ("Madam, I'm Adam") was a palindrome, a word or series of words which reads the same backward or forward (Greek *palindromos,* running back again). Time-honored examples are Goethals' cheeriest ("A man, a plan, a canal: Panama!"), Napoleon's weariest ("Able was I ere I saw Elba"), and middle-age's dreariest ("Sex at noon taxes"). The longest palindromic word in English is said to be *redivider,* the eccentric word on the list.*

All the other words are "emordnilaps," the word formed when *palindrome* is treated according to its definition and allowed to "run back" on itself. An impractically arcane contrivance? Not if you are one of the thousands of Americans who take the SAT, GRE, GMAT, or another college entrance examination. This question appeared on a recent exam:

Golf : flog :: Camus : ___?___
a. thrash
b. switch
c. vines
d. ivy
e. sumac

An important principle of test-taking was thus illustrated: when the associated pair of words seems absolutely unrelated, look for some trick connection. In the following analogy,

conflagration : ratio :: candlestick : ___?___
a. taper
b. lantern
c. lest
d. proportion
e. trick

a certain structural relationship—psychiatrists call it a clang association—pertains, as in a word's spelling something backward or, in this case, containing another word within itself.

---

*A contender for the longest palindromic proper name is *Malayalam,* an East Indian language.

"The difference between the right word and the almost right word is the difference between *lightning* and the *lightning bug.* " This observation by Mark Twain could be called an

epigone
epicure
epicene
epicrisis
epergne
epigram

The *Epigonoi* were the sons of the Seven against Thebes, who imitated their fathers by attacking Thebes. By this deed they lent their name to the generic *epigone,* "a second-rate imitator or follower," as of an artist or philosopher (Gk. *epigonos,* born after; from *epi- + gonos,* child). William F. Buckley, wordsmith par excellence, is fond of applying this pejorative to the Central American lackeys of Fidel Castro.

In the third century B.C. Epicurus pronounced sensuous pleasure to be the highest good (a sentiment with some modern analogues), supplying a name for Greek citizens devoted to sensuous pleasure and luxurious living. But the centuries have been kind to this word, so that nowadays an *epicure* isn't quite so crass, just a person with refined tastes for food and wine.

Time and usage have been even kinder to *epicene* (Gk. *epikoinos,* common to many, promiscuous, from *epi-,* to + *koinos,* common), for today the word is used to describe persons or objects having the characteristics of both the male and the female, as an epicene angel. Acknowledging that I look at our mod world through ever-aging eyes, I still would have to say that this adjective can be accurately applied to more of its denizens and their dress than ever before.

If you pronounce it ĭ-pĭk′-rĭ-sĭs, an *epicrisis* is the detailed critique of a literary work (Gk. *epi-,* over + *krinein,* to judge). With its customarily imperious hand, medicine coined *epicrisis* (Gk. *epi-,* after + *krisis,* crisis) and say ĕp′-ĭ-krī′-sĭs, "the crisis that comes after the primary crisis of the disease."

In the unhappy part of my life during which I was en-meshed in psychoanalysis, I dreamed that my wife turned into an *epergne,* a large silver or glass serving dish, usually branched and compartmented. At breakfast the next morn-ing, when I described her new form to her, she told me what an epergne was, else I might have forever remained ignorant. When I reported the dream to the analyst, he could make nothing of it. The origins of the word are just as obscure; the French *épargne* (saving) is believed to be the source, though nobody can explain just how "saving" became a serving dish. *The Oxford English Dictionary* points out—a little enigmati-cally, you'll agree—that the earliest epergnes seemed always to hold pickles. This is one of the many reassuring things about etymology: no matter how far you go, how deeply you dig, mystery remains.

Twain's pondering about the right word is, of course, an *epigram,* a concise and clever statement making a pointed ob-servation. Ole Samuel was famous for them, as fond of them as a subsequent but equally rugged American, Harry Truman, who kept his favorite Twain epigram on his White House desk: "Always do right. This will gratify some people, and astonish the rest."

Mark the one word in the list that does not go with all the other words:

Ping-Pong
borborygmi
cui cui
cuckoo
buzz
blimp

All but one of the words in the list are onomatopoeias (Gk. *onoma,* name + *poiēin,* to make), words that have the sound of their referents, like *pop, crack,* and *hiss.* Because of birds' cries, names of birds seem to find their way into this category very often, like *kiwi, killdeer,* and *cuckoo.* Most English speakers don't purse up their lips enough to sound much like a canary (Fr. *cui cui*), but the French do it for their children very well indeed.

Though it's come to be synonymous with table tennis, *Ping-Pong* is really a trademark for such sports equipment. And *borborygmi* are the rumblings and gurglings of an empty or unquiet stomach. The word is borrowed from medicine, a discipline not otherwise famous for artful naming. A list of onomatopoeias is a marvelous way to start a vocabulary notebook, or to add to the one you already have. Such a list ought to include some onomatopoeic possibilities of a more subtle nature, like *hobble, boomerang,* and *budgerigar.* An entertaining (albeit to my knowledge as yet unplayed) parlor game would be to present the pros and cons of why a particular word should or should not qualify for the list. My favorite onomatopoeia is *susurrus,* a soft whispering or rustling sound. You can almost hear it *murmur.*

The word that's not an onomatopoeia is *blimp.* The story goes that when aeronautical engineers began designing the first lighter-than-air craft, they experimented with an air sack outside a rigid metal skeleton. Finding this structure too heavy, they progressed to a boneless and compartmented balloon they called a *limp.* The first model, the *A-limp,* was unsuccessful, but—as you've already guessed—the second one worked fine.

Puggree, *jabot, trilby,* and *tangerine* are all

    breeds of dogs
    items of clothing
    weapons
    walking sticks
    varieties of fruit

An 1894 novel by George du Maurier has been largely forgotten except for two names from the book, two words that remain alive and well. Trilby O'Ferral models for Parisian artists until she falls under the spell of a sinister Hungarian voice coach named Svengali. Inspired by his hypnotic power, she becomes a singer, but she loses her talent when he dies. A forgettable story, perhaps, but the characters' names have outlived the tale: the stage play *Trilby* popularized the type of hat she wore, a soft felt with an indented crown, while *Svengali* became the word for any mesmeric seducer.

That scarf Stewart Granger always wrapped around his sun helmet for jungle movies is called a *puggree* (Hindi *pagrī,* turban). *Tangerine* is the black slang word for those orangy tan shoes with the pointed toes, like the ones Sportin' Life affected in *Porgy and Bess.*

My favorite teacher was a very old lady who wore a *jabot* so often that now I cannot imagine her without it. As with other articles of clothing like *epaulet, wristlet,* and *codpiece, jabot* comes from the portion of one's anatomy it covers (Fr. *gave,* throat), a cascade of frills down the front of a dress or shirt.

How would you rather be hanged?

> in effigy
> alfresco
> in mufti
> egregiously
> as a caitiff

Anyone who has a passion for words can remember a few examples in which he recalls exactly where he was or what he was doing when a particular word first came his way. An art lecturer, I remember well, used *alfresco* in describing Manet's *Le Déjeuner sur l'herbe,* that arresting painting of two fully dressed young men picnicking on the grass with a nude woman. Like the English phrase *of the clock,* which with usage became *o' the clock* and finally *o'clock,* the Italian *a il fresco* (in the fresh air, outdoors) was shortened to *al fresco* and ultimately to *alfresco.* An appropriate place for a hanging, but if you're the victim, any place is undesirable.

When JFK invited all the American Nobel prizewinners to dine with him in the White House, only William Faulkner declined, saying it was too far to travel for supper with strangers. A columnist I particularly like, reporting the incident, wrote that Faulkner could be *egregiously* (flagrantly, outstandingly) rude.*

In mufti means civilian dress (as worn by a military person), probably an obscure slang use of *mufti* as "a judge," originally one who interpreted Moslem religious law (Arabic *mufti,* one who decides).

A *caitiff* (Middle English *caitif,* prisoner, captive, wretch) is a base coward, a wretch who probably ought to be hanged—certainly an unenviable position.

The Latin *effigies* is the source for *effigy,* a crude image or dummy fashioned in the likeness of a person. It's bad to be portrayed like that, but not nearly so bad as being hanged, indoors or out.

Absit omen!, *zum gesund!,* and *Dieu vous benis!* are all exclamations or exhortations following

    adumbration
    lucubration
    salutation
    sternutation

Curious, that sternutation (sneezing) promotes benevolent comments like *Gesundheit!* and *Bless you!,* while other bodily symptoms (some a good deal more portentous) like coughing, snoring, belching, or vomiting invite no such response. That the soul issues from the nostrils and can do so with a sneeze—the

---

*At that meal Kennedy looked about the historic dining room and said that his guests were the greatest collection of American genius ever assembled there, "except possibly for when Thomas Jefferson dined here alone."

victim's eyes are always closed, mind you—was appreciated by
the Roman's *Absit omen!* ("Evil spirit be gone!") as well as the
Jewish mother, whose *zum gesund!* ("to health") was accompanied by an upward tug on her child's ear to prevent a catas-
trophic escape of his soul. A second sneeze would provoke a tug
on the other ear and a further admonition, *zum wachsen und
kwelln* ("to grow and thrive").

Selig Kavka* has further pointed out that Pope Gregory VII
recommended the "God bless you" in 619, after an Italian
pestilence brought death to some victims immediately after
they sneezed a few times. A children's game-song sounds an
ominous note from the plague years of the Middle Ages:

Ring around the rosy,	(the ring rash of plague)
Pocket full of posy,	(of hyssop, a fancied remedy)
Achew! Achew!	(nowadays "Ashes! Ashes!")
All fall down.	(dropping dead)

Isn't that a grim origin?

An *adumbration* is a foreshadowing (Latin *ad*, to + *umbra*,
shadow), while *lucubration* (L. *lucūbrāre*, to work at night by
lamplight) suggests laborious study or writing verging on pe-
dantry.

Salus (health) is the Latin word that has given the collective
word *salutation* to the "Dear Sirs" of our letters and the "Ladies and Gentlemen" of our speeches, as well as *salutary* and
salubrious (wholesome), to end on a healthful note.

---

*"The Sneeze—Blissful or Baneful," *Journal of the American Medical Association* 249
(17):2304–2305, May 6, 1983.

The words in the following list are known collectively as *contranyms.* What do they have in common?

cleave
scan
let
moot
wound up
commencement
handicap

In Genesis, the King James Version states that when a boy becomes a man, he will leave the house of his mother and father "and shall *cleave* unto his wife," meaning of course that the two will stick together. Ecclesiastes, upon the other hand, uses the same verb in a warning about splitting things up: "He that *cleaveth* wood shall be endangered." A contranym is a word with two (or more) contradictory meanings.

Scan, for example, can imply the most thorough sort of visual inspection, as in Pope's addition to Plutarch's caveat:

> Know thyself, presume not God to scan;
> The proper study of mankind is man.

Yet *scan* at another time can describe a reader's hasty and casual once-over of his morning newspaper.

Hamlet used *let* in its Elizabethan sense of "prevent":

> By heaven, I'll make a ghost of him that lets me,

the opposite* of today's meaning of *let:* "allow."

Depending upon how it is used, *moot* may mean either "debatable" or "no longer debatable." A clock that is *wound up* is ready to begin; a lecture about to be *wound up* is ending.

---

*Except in tennis's "*let* ball."

Commencement means one thing to a tyro and another to an academic, just as *handicapping* does to a golfer or a racing fan. The English language is replete with contranyms.

Which would you rather NOT be?

eupeptic
eudemonic
eurythmic
eulogized
euphoric

The Greek word *eus,* "good," shortened to the prefix *eu-,* has spawned two pages of words in any good English dictionary, in almost all cases the *eu-* indicating good, pleasant, or beneficial:* *eu-* + *peptic* (having good digestion), *demonic* (of good spirits), *rhythmic* (well-rhythmed), and *phoric* (of good bearing, happy). Good (*eu-*) words (Gk. *logos*) are spoken over the deceased in the form of a *eulogy,* something almost everybody would rather postpone, however *euphoniously* it might be delivered.

The foreign words in the list below have evolved (by usage and mispronunciation) into ordinary English words. Write the word in the blank at the right:

tempora (Portuguese) _____
bistrot (Russian) _____
decuria (Latin) _____
bangalo (Gujarati) _____

---

*Notable exceptions of non-obscure *eu-* words are *Europe* (Semitic "land of the setting sun") and *euchre* (origin unknown).

In his *Talking Your Way Around the World,* Mario Pei points out that the Japanese *tempura* arose from their Portuguese visitors' Lenten *tempora* (times), when the Europeans ate seafood rather than meat.

Though *Brewer's Dictionary of Phrase and Fable* cites the transliterated Russian *bistrot* (quick!) as a source (from the cries of 1815 soldiers in French restaurants) of *bistro,* the Poitou dialect *biste* (goat) and *bistouille* (the cheap whisky served there) may be more likely sources for the name of the modest French cafe.

In the aftermath of a more ancient war, Romans traded furs in sets of ten (L. *decuria*) with vanquished barbarians. Wilfred Funk shows how the resultant German *decher* reached English *dicker* through Middle English *dyker.* In America, where nouns so often and so quickly become verbs, a *dicker* of furs evolved into a word describing the bargaining over its value.

Bungalow is often reported to be an Anglicization of *Bangalore,* an Indian city where this sort of house is evidently popular. But *bangalo* in the Gujarati language means "of Bengal" and may thus be parent to both the place name and the architectural style.

What do these words have in common?

saturnalia, saturnine
mercurial
lunacy, lunatic
siriasis
influenza

One of man's many recurrent vanities is the notion that somehow the stars govern his actions, account for his behavior, or dictate his future. The idea is far from new. Romans who assigned Saturn as god of agriculture celebrated his day as a time of plenty, but the festivals degenerated into the sort of occasion that gave *saturnalia* its modern meaning: a period of unrestrained or orgiastic revelry and licentiousness. Somewhere along the way the god's name was also attached to the planet—sixth in order from the sun and thus remote, so that this heavenly body was later thought of as gloomy, cold, and aloof—the attributes gathered together in the meaning of the word *saturnine*. This is an occasion in which the same etymology is responsible for two similar words with quite dissimilar meanings, for *saturnalian* and *saturnine* imply very nearly opposite attitudes.

The planet smallest and nearest to the sun shares its name with the Roman god whose characteristics of swiftness, eloquence, and shrewdness are recalled in English usage. Shakespeare patterned Romeo's bright foil to suggest them all, then named him accordingly: *Mercutio.* Things and people who are quick and changeable in temperament are often called *mercurial.*

The conviction that mental derangement is associated with phases of the moon (L. *luna*) is no less ancient; the Romans' word for *lunatic* translates to English as "moonstruck" and has the same use as "crazy." Modern crime statistics and computers have illustrated that violent behavior is more common with a full moon than on a night with no moon, but the exact reason for this fact is as obscure to us as it was to Caesar.

Though Sirius is the brightest star in the sky, it won its etymological distinction not from its stellar intensity but from the observation that it rises with the sun in late summer. Though the "dog days" are often said to be named for the dogs who become rabid then, *siriasis* (heat stroke) actually got its name from accompanying the Dog Star (L. *Canicula*), another name for Sirius.

When I used to practice medicine and see seventy sick children on those awful January days, I never had enough time to wonder just what malignant *influence* made them ill. Italians of two centuries ago were surer than I: they believed the 1743 epidemic of grippe was due to "intangible visitation," *influenza*, from the stars.

Each definition below is represented by a word that has the sound of a single letter of the English alphabet. Insert the letter in the blank at the left of each definition.

_____ the pigtail in the hair of a bullfighter
_____ the second person singular pronoun
_____ the bud on a twig or tuber
_____ the official seat or office of a bishop
_____ a small island
_____ "Turn right, horse!"
_____ the second person plural pronoun
_____ the relative calm at the center of a cyclone
_____ a wing of a building at right angles with the main structure
_____ an afternoon social

Give yourself bonus points if you saw the acrostic and recognized that it's what you should get when you idle away your time with word games: *queue, you, eye, see, cay, gee, you, eye, ell, tea.*

Which one of these words still means about the same thing as it meant 150 years ago?

professional (noun)
chauvinism
venereal
parameter
dyke (a female homosexual)

Only a generation ago the *professions* were law, medicine, and the clergy, and those who held a position in one of these was a *professional.* Nowadays (aside from sports usage, to differentiate a paid player from an amateur) the term is much broader. Because the adjective seems to lend dignity to any sort of occupation it describes, *professional* has been so watered down through usage that now it means little more than "competent." The laborers who move your household goods are accordingly billed as "the real professionals."

Nicholas Chauvin (fl. 1815) devoted himself so faithfully and so uncritically to Napoleon that his surname became synonymous with militant patriotism. Much wounded but little decorated, super-soldier Chauvin was rewarded with only a red ribbon and the meager pension of 200 francs a year, but he nevertheless continued to wax eloquent upon the heroism and generosity of the Little Corporal. A popular 1831 stage entertainment used his name to personify his fanatical patriotism, and the character later appeared in Orczy's *The Scarlet Pimpernel.* But in our time feminism has stripped away these earlier historical connotations, so that now *chauvinist* (almost always preceded by *male* and succeeded by *pig*) is very nearly the same as *sexist.*

The Roman goddess of love and beauty, analogue to the Greek Aphrodite, has generated half a page of words about love, through the Latin *venerāri,* from *Venus.* From "profound respect or reverence" *(veneration)* to that outthrust at the base of a woman's abdomen (*mons veneris,* "love hill"), all the *Venus* words at one time suggested romantic or reverential love; *venereal* once meant simply "loving." George Peele chose *Venelia* for the name of his loving heroine in *The Old Wives' Tale* (1595). Today the range of implications of this adjective has contracted rather than expanded, with *venereal* used for nothing other than to describe a variety of diseases with distinctly unromantic and disreputable associations.

Parameter originally meant "a variable or arbitrary constant appearing in a mathematical expression, each value of which restricts or determines the specific forms of the expression." The journal *Verbatim* tells how *parameter* has been kidnapped into the patois of all sorts of disciplines, each time with a different meaning. For example, in economics we hear, "Confine yourself to the parameters [meaning the "limits"] of the established budgets." In medicine, "The patient's diagnosis may be verified by multiple parameters [systems of measurements] available in the lab." In politics, "Difference of opinion is a parameter [characteristic, defining element] of the democratic system." And in law, "We must define the parameters [standards] of responsibility one case at a time." All these variants illustrate arcane and jargonized misuse of the once-specific mathematical term *parameter.*

This leaves us only with *dyke,* a female homosexual. Though seemingly new to many a pair of old ears, this truncation of *dike-jumper* has enjoyed more than sesquicentennial use as a term for one who has crossed a sexual boundary into a different field.

The use of *gay* for the male homosexual is yet older. In Shakespeare's time the Elizabethan theater allowed only male players, show business being too wicked for women. The young men who played the parts of women and girls were known as the *gaieties,* and usage contracted the term, just as it did *dike-jumper,* to our present *gay.*

B*ooboisie, hoi polloi, ruck,* and *canaille* are all

gourmet dishes
social classes
odds and ends
criminals

H. L. Mencken coined the portmanteau word *booboisie (boob + bourgeoisie)* to describe that class of the population composed of the stupid and the gullible. He opined that chiropractors are not to be denigrated, for they perform a eugenic function by killing off only the *booboisie.*

The Greek *hoi polloi,* "the many," and the Middle English *ruke,* "a stack," suggest the teeming, untutored rabble of nonpropertied classes, as does *canaille,* from the Italian *canaglia,* "a pack of dogs." All the terms are invariably applied contemptuously.

Wʜat do these words have in common?

codswallop
bunk
balderdash
hogwash
folderol

Many etymologists discreetly omit the possibility of any testicular origins for *codswallop* (*cod*, scrotum). They also overlook the obsolete verb *codd* (to fool or buff a person) and instead cite nineteenth-century inventor Hiram Codd's bottle closure for his own *wallop* (once "a blow" but by Codd's time "mild beer"), with only a minor discourtesy to one of his *d*'s. Perhaps his design was defective or his beverage somehow fraudulent, for in some way *cod's wallop* and then *codswallop* became the word to describe ideas or statements that are thought to be foolishness.

Fifty years before Hiram and his ill-fated bottle top, the Missouri Compromise was under debate in the House of Representatives. Deeply enmeshed in this complex issue, the members were surprised and annoyed when the representative from Buncombe County, North Carolina, took the floor and launched a rambling and irrelevant speech about his hometown. Some members walked out in disgust, and when those who remained complained, the speaker apologized, "I'm talking for Buncombe." He might as well have omitted the word *for* in his sentence right then and there, because by 1828 *talking for Bunkum* meant talking nonsense. Usage shortened this pejoration to *bunk,* and since about 1920 the useful negative *debunk* has enjoyed popular and less informal use.

The American Heritage Dictionary of the English Language dismisses *balderdash* as "origin unknown," but anyone who's ever drunk a glass of the noisome stuff will probably agree that the notion of mixing beer and milk is so readily identifiable as nonsense that explanations are hardly necessary. *Shandygaff* (beer and lemonade) isn't quite as unpalatable, and *shandy* itself means about the same thing as "eccentric," or maybe "giddy," so it falls into a nearby category.

American folk expressions using *hog* are numerous enough to require two full pages in *Brewer's Dictionary of Phrase and Fable,* and Charles Funk's *A Hog on Ice* (1950) discusses this and other *hog* phrases at considerable length. A good case could be made that people simply like the sound of the word, the brevity and strength of it. The etymology for *hogwash* is itself brief; "the swill or garbage fed to hogs" had but a short trip in order to become "waste words, nonsense."

Browning's *Mr. Sludge* typifies the meaningless refrain in a song when he sings

> Fol-de-rol-de-rido
> Liddle iddle-ol,

and the Limelighters intone

> Hey li-lee li-lee,
> Hey li-lee, li lee lo.

In the American West the term *folderol* (also *falderol* and *fal de rol**) required only a short time to become said nonsense as well as sung nonsense. An analogue in verse is the combination of meaningless syllables in the sailors' "Yo-ho-ho and a bottle of rum," called a *rumbelow.*

---

*French *rôler:* to spin out legal documents (to increase the costs).

$\mathbf{P}$ick out the one term in the list that does not go with all the others:

antigodlin
antimacassar
antiwalkus
cattywampus
antigoglin

Each term except *antimacassar* is a regional expression for the same thing, and each of them is a good example of the observation that folk terms don't always arise because they are easier ways to say a hard word: *diagonal* really isn't difficult to say.

Macassar is a Celebes town of Indonesia, undistinguished except as the exporter of an oil used in a popular nineteenth-century pomade.* A domestic accomplishment of every Victorian gentlewoman was the crocheting of ornate doilies to protect her chair cushions from this ointment. This particular item of linen received its name not because the ladies had anything against the Indonesian city, but only because it protected the furniture from grease spots. The arrival of the "dry look" in men's coiffures was good news for hair stylists and manufacturers of spray-can propellant, but it was bad for hatters and makers of pomade. The word itself seems to have been another casualty from those halcyon times: nowadays very few people under thirty years old recognize *antimacassar.*

---

*Hair oil got the name *pomade* because the original stuff was apple-scented (Italian *pomo*, apple).

Bodacious

is an American slang word
is a portmanteau word
means intrepid
is a restaurant in Mt. Pleasant, Texas
means brave and fearless

Bodacious thrust itself into American slang* with the vigor of all good portmanteau words—the sound of it somehow ringing mightier than the sum of its parts *(bold + audacious)*. Whether the East Texas restaurant by the same name expects you to associate its title with their bold decor (defunct license plates and a collection of specimens of barbed wire) or the authoritative taste of their food (spicy barbecue and four-alarm chili) is less than clear, but the place has been popular for a long time. Certainly *bodacious* encompasses brave, fearless, and intrepid as well.

The word that goes with *autumnal, vernal,* and *hibernal* is

auroral
austral
cryptic
melancholic
estival

---

*Some philologists maintain that *slang* is itself a portmanteau word *(slovenly + language)*. Whether this is correct or not, the description may be appropriate: ask any fifteen-year-old for fine distinctions among *geek, dork, nub,* and *nerd,* and you'll find as much imprecision as the word *slang* implies.

I never understood the redundancy in Herman Wouk's 1947 novel he called *Aurora Dawn*. The Roman goddess of the dawn was Aurora, and sometimes in poetry the adjective is *aurorean* instead of *auroral*, but both words mean "pertaining to or resembling the dawn." *Dawn Dawn?*

The northern lights *(aurora borealis)* have a counterpart in the southern sky, called *aurora australis*. The Latin word *auster*, "south," gave us the name for this phenomenon, as well as for the southern island continent Australia and numerous other places from Austerlitz to Austin and for the god of the south wind *(Auster)*.

The Greek *kryptikos*, "cryptic," sounds as if it means "hidden," having that sort of sinister ring about it, so that *cryptogram* (coded message) and *cryptonym* (secret name) possess an underground mystery of their own. My favorite is *cryptogenic*, a sort of "I give up" doctors' word applied to a disease of unknown origin (the medical school lecturer who introduced this word to me said that the definition of *cryptogenic* is "I don't know"). For centuries physicians have recognized their patients' discomfort with *cryptogenic*, undiagnosed disorders. Craftier practitioners have for decades recognized and applied the Rumpelstiltskin Principle (i.e., "naming a thing makes it get better"), so that when a frustrated victim of some unnamed disease asks his sixth doctor for a diagnosis and is promptly told that he's suffering from phenylpyruvic oligophrenia or pneumonoultramicroscopicsilicovolcanokoniosis, he says, "Thank God!"

Centuries before the existence of such medical sophistications, a doctor treated a patient according to how much out-of-kilter the patient's humors were perceived to be. Medieval medicine credited imbalances of blood, phlegm, and bile as the causes of illness, but these early theories thankfully left behind them little more useful than their corresponding adjectives *sanguine, phlegmatic,* and *bilious.* A superfluity of black (Gk. *melan*) bile (Gk. *kholē*) precipitated the particularly noxious disorder of pathological depression (melancholia); *melancholic* still means gloomy or depressed—regardless of the patient's level of black bile.

Do people *estivate,* just as bears *hibernate?* Yes indeed, and the verb implies that they summer (L. *aestivus*) in a state of dormancy. *Estival* complements the remaining adjectives for the three seasons of autumn, spring, and winter.

Pick out the one word in the list that is out of place:

zwieback
frown
armored cow
smores
marcel

Before the days when a young mother could buy ready-to-gnaw packages of teething biscuits at the grocery store, she made her own, toasting thin slices of bread. Perhaps a German housewife was the first to describe the process: German *zwie,* twice + *backen,* to bake.

Such inconveniences of the good old days were ameliorated a bit by the ubiquitous soda fountain, where you might while away a summer afternoon by ordering up eccentric mixtures from an obliging soda jerk. One such concoction was known as a *frown,* a mixture of Coca-Cola and lemon extract that unquestionably produced a grimace from the taster. Similarly, the horticulturist who named the *nasturtium* (L. *nasus,* nose + *torquēre,* to twist) reported a similar reaction to the pungent taste of the plant. The most curious of these is the origin of a *sardonic* expression. This lip-curled cynicism resulted from eating the "Sardinian herb," a bitter and poisonous plant supposed to distort the face of the eater.

Armored cow is canned milk in the argot of the military, those rough-and-ready wordsmiths who gave the world *pogey bait* for free food, *battery acid* for bad coffee, and *S.O.S.* (ask any veteran if you don't know) for chipped beef on toast.

Those adults fortunate (or unfortunate) enough to have been exposed to the cuisine of a Girl Scout wiener roast probably recognize the fine points of preparing something called *smores.* A graham cracker is topped with a square of Hershey bar and a marshmallow that has been heated well beyond the melting point. Partakers of this amalgam are said invariably to smack their lips and call for "s'more."

This leaves us with the only indisputably inedible item on the list, the *marcel,* a hairdo devised by the eponymous Marcel Grateau (died 1936), a French hairdresser. Watching an old TV movie the other night, I found myself a little disconcerted to see Mary, Queen of Scots wearing a marcel, some 400 years before M. Grateau made his mark as a coiffeur, corroborating yet one more time the axiom that one shouldn't expect too much from old motion pictures.

In the list below are four names and a sentence, each of which has been shortened by usage into a single English word. Supply the word for each.

"God be with you." _____
Saint Claire _____
Mary Magdalene _____
Saint Audrey's lace _____
Saint Mary of Bethlehem _____

How many times was "God be with you" uttered before it was contracted to *good-bye*? And isn't it curious (and tiresome) that the civilization that shortened these words and phrases is the same one that has lengthened *reduplication, irregardless, effectuate,* and *orientate*? It's a long way from *in this time frame* to *now*.

While *Saint Claire* survived a short and unemotional transition to the American surname *Sinclair,* the name of Mary Magdalene endured a sad journey. Reformed by Christ and rid of her evil ways, she was so often depicted by painters as a penitent with tear-stained face and swollen eyes that her name—by now shortened to *maudlin*—became synonymous with those who weep too easily. The English college that the American reader recognizes as *Magdalene* is pronounced *maudlin* by the British speaker. Usage and history have been as unkind to this noble biblical woman as they have been to Hector, for the name of the mightiest Trojan warrior of them all has inexplicably come to mean "bully."

The tale of Saint Audrey of Ely is little happier than poor Mary's. Widowed at an early age, this seventh-century daughter of King Anna of East Anglia repaired to a convent when her second marriage to a boy prince failed. Soon after endowing a monastery on her island of Ely in 672, Audrey developed a breast tumor which she attributed to necklaces of precious stones. Because her story was a famous one at the time, wearing silk necklace substitutes became popular, and St. Audrey's Fairs each June 23 (her death date) specialized in selling inexpensive necklaces. Elision of her name led to the descriptive word for such costume jewelry and other cheap things: *tawdry.*

The Saint Mary of Bethlehem Hospital began as a priory in 1242 and became a lunatic asylum in 1377. Given to the City of London by Henry VIII, Bethlehem (by then known as *Bedlem*) fell victim to an inhumane sort of hucksterism; in 1676 anyone might pay two pence to "gaze upon the inmates"—and bait them with rocks and sticks, if he so desired. The resultant noise and outcry became *bedlam,* the epitome of uproar and confusion. Today's Bethlehem is a war museum outside Bishopsgate in southeast London. Now sedate and a little shabby, this eponymous structure is little reminiscent of the horrors once perpetrated within its walls that made its name a synonym for chaos.

A *kickshaw* is

> a fancy dish in cookery
> something dainty or elegant but unsubstantial
> a fantastical, frivolous person
> an Anglicization of a French phrase

The next time your British friends ridicule some Americanization of an English word, remind them (but do it gently) of what they have done to French. It's hard to believe that *kick-shaw* was once *quelque chose* (something). You can supplement your observation with *Route de Roi,* once the King's Highway in French, but now only *Rotten Row* in English. Sometimes Frenchmen have deserved it: their Anglophobic slur-word for toilet is *lieu à l'anglaise,* "English place," which the British have shortened to *loo* and consider it pejorative to the French. Each of the four answers is correct.

But, as I warned, remind them gently, for many Britishers are fond of etymology, too, and they may in turn point out what French corruptions the Yanks themselves have committed. Look at how usage in the American South has altered these once-French place names:

> *Chemin Couvert* (shady lane)—Smackover, Arkansas
> *Purgatoire* (purgatory)—Picketwire (river), Arkansas
> *Bonne Terre* (beautiful earth)—Bonnie Tar, Missouri
> *L'eau Frais* (fresh water)—Low Freight, Arkansas
> *Glaise à Paul* (Paul's land)—Glazypool, Arkansas, and
>   Glacierpool, Louisiana

The name for each of these storied birds has acquired an additional meaning. Write the non-avian definition beside each bird:

> albatross
> pica
> icterus
> phoenix
> halcyon

Misfortune has dogged the name of the *albatross* in much the same way the ill-fated bird hounded and haunted the Ancient

Mariner. *Albatross* came to mean "any handicap, constant burden, or heavy cross to bear" when Coleridge's seaman shot the bird with a crossbow and had to wear the carcass around his neck in penance. Even *alcatraz* (pelican), the Portugese origin of the word, took on formidable overtones when the San Francisco Bay island by that name became for awhile the site of a federal prison. Its very name struck fear into the heart of any convict unfortunate enough to be banished to it.

Pica is the term for the sort of craving for unnatural food that one is likely to experience in pregnancy or hysteria. (*Hysteria* got its name because ancient physicians assigned the womb as a source of all madness.) *Pica,* the Latin word that became the Middle English *pie,* meaning the magpie bird, assumed its extra-avian connotations from that bird's omnivorous nature, just as *cormorant* came to mean any greedy or rapacious person. *Magpie* as "a person who chatters" was built from *Mag* (a pet form of *Margaret* and a dialectal name for a chatterbox in proverbs) + *pie.*

Ancient men of medicine figured in the lexical progeny of the *icterus,* too. Shamans have told us of this little white bird that perches on the bedpost of every patient suffering from jaundice. In the course of recovery, as the victim's skin returns to its normal color, the bird turns yellow and flies away. A remedy with which to treat jaundice is thus an *icteric,* and jaundice itself is called *icterus.*

The origin of *phoenix* stretches back even further, into the dawn of Egyptian mythology. This bird was reputed to consume itself by fire every five hundred years, then rise rejuvenated from its own ashes. The extended meaning of *phoenix* rose with the story of this immortal bird: something of unsurpassed excellence or beauty, a paragon.

Halcyon brings us the most lyrical of bird stories. This mythical avian, identified with the kingfisher, reputedly had the power to calm the wind and the waves during the winter solstice while it nested on the sea, so that *halcyon* is now an adjective identified with tranquility, with peace and calm. The *halcyon days* are days of fine weather occurring near the winter solstice, especially the seven days before and the seven after, attributed to the bird's magical calming powers.

Sinistral is the opposite of

    dextral
    adroit
    augural
    auspicious
    vestiary

With rhetorical indignation Wilfred Funk ponders just who's responsible for crediting the right (L. *dexter*) with good things and the left (L. *sinister*) with those unwholesome. The associations of *leftist* are as unsavory as those of *righteous* are moral; a "left-handed oath" is not binding, and "the right foot foremost" assures the superstitious man a safe entrance. *Dexterity* is a most agreeable attribute, and who would want to be "ambisinistral"? Even the recalcitrant French for once agree (*à droit*, to the right; *gauche*, left).

The phrase "the right foot foremost" points toward an answer, for it was ancient Rome where every palazzo featured a front-door servant to be sure every guest entered with his right foot.

It all goes back to the Romans. No surprise there, because their language has provided us with a startling 50 percent of the words we use. The *augurs* were Roman religious officials who undertook to read the signs *(auspicium,* source of English *auspice)* of the gods to decide whether the deities were favorable or not to a proposed course of action. In Rome the augurs were always consulted before any important public action was taken. Their activities have generated the English words *augur, augural, inaugurate,* and *auspicious*—and also generated the disfavor for the left side of things, for in augury, signs (e.g., birds) appearing on the left forboded evil, while right-sided signs *augured* well. Plutarch said that the west (left side of the augur) was toward the setting—departing—sun and thus ill-omened.

Of course each member of the college of augurs wore vestments (from L. *vestis,* garment) suitable to his prophetic office; from this same root came our word *vestiary,* the room containing the clothes worn on particular occasions.

What do these words have in common?

salmagundi
olla podrida
potpourri
farrago
gallimaufry

It was the French, perennial masters of haute cuisine, who devised *salmagundi* (Fr. *salmigondis*), a salad of chopped meat, anchovies, eggs, and onions, served on lettuce with vinegar and oil. Texans concocted a similar salad with a similarly reckless name, *slangjang,* in the same spirit of mixing such incongruous foods. Thus by extension a *salmagundi* became any mixture or assortment. In this second sense, the word was used for Washington Irving's humorous periodical which he called *Salmagundi; or The Whim-Whams and Opinions of Launcelot Langstaff, Esq. and Others* (1807–1808), while William Faulkner's *Salmagundi* was a potboiler of hodgepodge poetry and criticism.

The analogous Spanish dish is less elegant; *olla podrida* (Sp., "rotten pot") is nothing fancier than a well-seasoned stew of vegetables and meat, but its nature again suggested a miscellany, so that *olla podrida* can also mean any assorted mixture. From the same "rotten pot" the French produced *potpourri,* a combination of various unrelated elements (like rose petals and spices).

Farrago in the sense the Romans used it ("an assortment of grains mixed for animal fodder") is seldom heard, for nowadays a *farrago* is a medley, a conglomeration, a mixture—from Virginia Woolf's "farrago of absurdities" to P. Meyer's descriptive word for the IRS form 1040.

Only a little less unappetizing (albeit still Gallic in origin) is the humble French hash made from yesterday's random leftovers. *Gallimaufry*'s etymology is as inelegant as the dish itself (Fr. *galer,* to live a merry life + *mafrer,* to eat voraciously), but its name has also been duly extended to mean "a jumble, a mishmash." Further examples in which the word for various food mixtures has come to mean a random assortment of anything are *pastiche, olio,* and *pasticcio.*

Draw these words:

ampersand _____
macron _____
virgule _____
grave _____
ankh _____

The old-fashioned schoolchild's recitation of letters and symbols always began "A *per se* a" and ended with "And *per se* and," meaning "& (the sign) by itself (equals) and." A simple contraction produced *ampersand*.

The little horizontal line above a vowel called a *macron* indicates that it's pronounced the same as when we say the letter by itself: *stātus quō*. A mathematician's *vinculum* (meaning "treat as a single term") is long enough to cover two letters *(ōō)*.

Commoner names for *virgule* (L. *virgula,* small rod) are *slash, shilling,* and *solidus,* depending upon where you live—or sometimes depending upon whether it means "per" (e.g., miles/hour), or "or" (his/her), or indicates verse line-ends in text ("Candy / Is dandy").

A *grave* marks a letter to be articulated toward the back of the throat (*Sèvres*), or, as in Italian (*città*), it can mark stress. An *acute* goes the other way and also affects pronunciation (*bon appétit*) or indicates stress.

The *ankh* or *ansate cross* is simply a T with a loop or handle (L. *ansa*), so that anything with a handle is *ansated*: ⚲

Visual, aural, gustatory, olfactory, and

haptic
lachrymal
dysgeusic
mephitic
xenophilic

Those adjectives that pertain to the senses of sight, sound, taste, and smell are complemented by *haptic* (Gk., touch), a word that's useful when you want to describe a person who relishes tactile sensations, but you know that *touchy* means something else.

The Latin *lacrima* (tears) fathered English *lachrymal*, "of the tears or the glands that produce them"—as well as *lachrymator* (tear gas), *lachrymatory* (a vase for tears), and the curious name for a wine called *Lacrima Cristi* (literally, "tears of Christ"). *Lachrymose* has undergone a process linguists call pejoration, where the semantic status of a word is lowered with usage over a period of time; once meaning simply "tearful, inclined to weep," *lachrymose* now most often implies maudlin sentimentality. Another example of pejoration in this special linguistic sense is *egregious,* which began as "distinguished or remarkable" and ended as "flagrantly bad." Rather like poor Hector.

Dysgeusic was the lugubrious condition of Tom Lehrer's army mess sergeant, who was unfortunate enough to have had "his taste buds shot off in the war." An even sadder circumstance would be to have one's name immortalized as a word for "foul-smelling," a fate hardly deserved by the devil himself. But it is so: Mephistopheles, the devil to whom Faust sold his soul, begat *mephitic* as just such a term.

Xenophobic describes a characteristic of most two-year-olds, who because of separation anxieties are fearful *(-phobic)* of the stranger (Gk. *xenos*). A baby under a year old is most often the opposite, personifying one with a strong affinity *(-phile)* for a novel face: *xenophilic.*

The roots and stems of the last ten questions have provided the foundations for a favorite word of the really hard-core logophile. *Melcryptovestimentaphiliac* is one of the most colorful and specific words of our time. A hard word to work into a conversation? Here's a true situation in which the word would have found *exact* use:

A year ago a close friend of mine fell upon a sad duty. A widowed and childless aunt had died, and my friend and a distant cousin were dispatched to her home to dispose of her possessions. Because Aunt Neda had been the retiring and modest wife of a staid country minister, they were more than a little surprised to encounter a large drawer full of frilly black underwear, some of it still packaged and unworn. While the two women were debating about what to do with this unexpected discovery, an aged brother of the deceased appeared and said with evident relish that he would take it off their hands. If my friend had been suitably prepared for this once-in-a-lifetime opportunity, she could have said with great precision, "Why, Uncle! I didn't know you were a melcryptovestimentaphiliac."

All these words but one are considered, *historically speaking,* to be lascivious or "dirty." Circle the eccentric word.

jazz
dugs
fico
crapper
pornoseptuagenarian
callipygian
genuglyphics
infibulate
parnel

It is seldom in linguistic history that the advent of so large and so old a segment of the language can be dated with accuracy, but the birth year of vulgar words can be set with precision: 1066. Of course that was the year William of Normandy conquered the Anglo-Saxons and became King William I of England. Among many novelties imported to the new court was the adoption of Norman French as the official language. It was thus that in England, French became the language of the gentle, the noble, the fashionable. Before 1066 the infamous four-letter, Anglo-Saxon words for body parts and functions were not infamous; they were used without prejudice by everybody, lord and lady, serf and servant. Suddenly only the yokels and the illiterate used them, so that they became *vulgar* (L., of the people).

Did you pick *jazz* as a candidate for the only "clean" word? It's historically the dirtiest word on the list. At one time synonymous with that choicest of all profanities *(fuck),* the word was cleaned up after its use in connection with that most American of music forms. One authority opines that the word originally described that music played (discreetly and behind a curtain) in New Orleans brothels, that *jazz music* was subsequently shortened to *jazz.* A famous old low-down Dixieland* tune is entitled "Jazz Me," with unsubtle implications, and in *The Confessions of Nat Turner,* William Styron left no doubt when he had an uppity black youth fantasize dangerously about "jazzin' that white pussy." Nothing historically clean about *jazz.*

One of the methods Hamlet used to convince his family and friends that he was going mad was to change his character by talking dirty. He used the Elizabethan profanity for "breast" when he described the tediously agreeable and compliant courtier, Osric: "He did comply with his dug [tit] before he sucked it."

When Nixon got off the plane in Argentina, brandishing his famous spread-finger salute with both hands, he didn't know at the time that his victory signal was dangerously close to the Argentinians' gesture of contempt *(fico),* and he must have wondered about the sudden cooling of his reception. An analogous scene might be Deng Xiaoping stepping off the Washington plane and waving to the crowd with his middle fingers upthrust. The press would lose no time in dismissing the Chinese dictator as merely a dirty old man *(pornoseptuagenarian).*

Among all the nice words beginning with *calli-* (from Gk. *kalli-,* beautiful), like *calliope* (-voice), *calligraphy* (-writing)

---

*Exactly where geographically is the heart of *Dixie*? Nobody really knows, but the best theory is based upon the etymology of the word: nineteenth-century currency from the Bank of Louisiana was imprinted DIX FRANCS and called *Dixies* by river traders, so that a good case can be made for the Mississippi River basin as the heart of Dixie.

and *calliopsis* (-appearance), hunkers *callipygian* (having beautiful buttocks), a word indubitably lascivious in flavor—yet somewhat more likely to find conversational use than *melcryptovestamentaphiliac.*

I must take issue with one word in the definition of the term *genuglyphics:* "the practice of decorating the female knees in order to make them more erotic." Of course it's the "more" that troubles me, and I think you may agree. In any case, you're unlikely to have your sensibilities offended by hearing it spoken very often. The same relative obsolescence applies to the only verb on the list besides *jazz;* to *infibulate* is "to fit with a chastity belt."

Even the OED agrees that a *parnel* is the mistress of a priest, but no finger is pointed to an original guilty woman (though *Parnel* is a common Irish surname); the term seems to have been illicit from the start.

In contrast to *jazz,* a word cleaned up with time and usage, the surname of Thomas Crapper has suffered soiling so intense that this sanitary engineer and inventor of Crapper's Valveless Water Waste Preventor (the flush toilet) has often been erroneously renamed John Crapper by overzealous word-mongers who point out that usage has desecrated the poor Victorian's first name as well, employing it too as another name for "lavatory."

Match the word on the left in the following list with its definition on the right.

canary	like a dog
sycophant	fig-shower
pansy	thought
bellibone	fair and good
dandelion	feline dentition
salt	military wages
calculus	cab fare
sabotage	pertaining to shoes
colporteur	a Bible salesman
alienist	a psychiatrist

How far down the list did you get before discovering that the words and their definitions are already arranged appropriately and need no unscrambling? *Canary* illustrates that reducing a word to its Latin root is not invariably definitive. The Spanish named the Atlantic island group *Islas Canarias* (Isles of Dogs) from the large dogs *(canes)* once bred there, and it was much later that the little songbird from the Canaries was introduced to Europe under the name of its original home. Even common names can be deceptive.

A *sycophant* (Gk. *sykophantēs,* fig-shower) as one who wins favor by aiding or flattering influential persons (e.g., kings) was first personified by those who denounced the king's enemies by showing the vulgar and accusatory gesture called "the fig" (the raised fist with the thumb between first and second fingers*).

The next three words on the list are more Anglicizations of

---
*Italian *fica,* vulva.

French words and phrases. Even in the grip of impending madness, Ophelia translates *pansy* helpfully:

> There's rosemary, that's for remembrance;
> pray, love, remember: and there is pansies,
> that's for thoughts.

The French *pensée* (thought) had become *pansy* to the Elizabethan tongue, just as the elegant dance step, *chassé,* has declined to the hasty *sashay* of modern English. In *Popllies and Bellibones/A Celebration of Lost Words,* Susan Sperling explains that the discordant and anatomically improbable *bellibone* was once the sunny French phrase *belle et bonne* (fair and good). And it's the saw-toothed leaves of the *dandelion* that suggest lion's teeth (Fr. *dents de lion*), rather than the pesky flower itself.

Your *salary* is the remnant of the Roman soldier's *salarium* (salt allowance), once given to him to buy this indispensable commodity (L. *sal*); "He isn't worth his salt" is a quip that harks back to classical times. It was also those resourceful Romans who devised the first meter for a taxi,* a perforated container of pebbles (L. *calculi*) arranged so that the rotating chariot wheel shook them out at a regular rate. When you arrived at your destination, the *calculus* was the fare you paid.

Was the first industrial saboteur an enterprising vandal who put his shoe (Fr. *sabot*) into his machine to jimmy the works and impede production? Maybe. French *saboter* (to clatter shoes) still means "to work clumsily," and the sabot, a shoe carved from a single piece of wood, is nothing if not clumsy.

Colporteur ought to mean "Nightish and Dayish," but it doesn't. This word for the itinerant peddler (Fr. *comporteur*) of

---

*Later *taximeter cabriolet* (literally, "wild goat," because it bounced like one).

devotional literature conveys the picture of a drummer encumbered by a book satchel with a neck (Fr. *col*) strap to support the load.

Inmates of French mental hospitals were once *aliénés,* and those who treated them *aliénistes* (English *alienists,* psychiatrists), but now the term is used specifically for a psychiatrist accepted by a court as an expert on mental competence.

The state of Miss Havisham's rooms in *Great Expectations* (where she is found thirty years after she had been jilted at her wedding) could with greatest precision be described as

aulic
august
avuncular
augean
au gratin

Though *The American Heritage Dictionary* suggests that *jilt* is derived from *jill** (girl), who is thus eponymic (though unnamed), a more likely source would be from the French *faire gille,* which means "to run away."

From the Greek *aulē* (court) comes *aulic,* courtly, pertaining to a royal court. Miss Havisham's dusty rooms and rotting bridal gown suggest nothing of such elegance, nor did they inspire awe or admiration *(august).* No doubt that marauding mice had scattered her moldy wedding cake, but "covered with bread crumbs and cheese" *(au gratin)* is far from an accurate

---

*Also *Gill* (girl, sweetheart), short for *Gillian, Jillian,* the Anglicized form of *Juiliana.*

description of the rooms. Even if her room might be considered a metaphor for her long career of revenge and retribution, it could never be described as *avuncular* (like a benevolent uncle).

The sixth of the twelve labors of Hercules was to clean in a single day the stables of Augeas, filled with three thousand cattle and unmucked for thirty years. He did it by diverting two rivers to wash away the colossal mess. Miss Havisham's rooms had accumulated dust and soil for a like period of time, so that no better word could describe their state: *augean.*

A young woman in a pretty summer frock goes well with a

gazebo
gazabo
gigolo
fandango
Bordeaux

The romantic intimations of a pavilion or belvedere *(gazebo),* a summerhouse or open, roofed gallery, almost demand ornamentation with an attractively dressed young woman, and an accompanying lad *(gazabo)* would not be inappropriate, even if he were kept by her as a lover *(gigolo).* An animated and fast Spanish dance in triple time *(fandango)* requires at least two such participants, who might plausibly refresh themselves after this disportation with a glass of *Bordeaux,* red or white wine from regions near that French seaport city.

I*shmael, pariah,* and *ostracism* all suggest

Moby Dick
initiation procedures
Biblical tribes
royalty
dismissal

In Genesis—a marvelous book, mind you, whether you're religious or not—Moses describes how Sarai (meaning "my princess"), childless wife of Abram (whose name means "exalted father") overcame her infertility by giving her handmaid Hagar (meaning "flight") to her husband as a concubine. The servant is delivered of a baby with evident hope, for he is adopted by Abram and named *Ishmael* ("may God hear").

But this story of surrogate motherhood is soon complicated: Sarai herself becomes pregnant and subsequently gives birth to Isaac ("laughter"—which is what she got from her friends when ninety-year-old Sarai announced she was expecting). Following Isaac's birth, the spelling of his parents' names is changed—without comment from the author—to reflect the gravity of the event: now *Sarai* becomes the more-familiar name *Sarah* ("princess for all the race"), and the name *Abram* is lengthened to *Abraham* ("father of a multitude").

This leaves no place in the tribe for Ishmael, who with his mother Hagar is dismissed to the desert, destined to become the quintessential wanderer (and prime ancestor of the Arab people, via his twelve sons). It is thus that his name has become synonymous with "outcast."

In the language of Tamil a *paraiyan* was once a drummer, an occupation not originally déclassé, but *Pariahs* later became members of one of the lower castes of India. Europeans extended the term to those of no class at all, so that in modern usage it is applied to outcasts generally.

In a ceremony which included a popular vote ancient Athenians cast out citizens considered dangerous to the state. This poll was taken when each voting member signified his position with a shard or shell (Gk. *ostrakon*) to indicate his vote against the outcast member, who was thereby banished by *ostracism.*

With which of the following would you prefer to be involved?

defalcation
defeneration
defenestration
defossion
decollation
deosculation

Among the plethora of synonyms for theft of various sorts, *embezzlement* is accompanied by just two. *Defalcation* is one of these, from the Latin root meaning "to cut off." Perhaps *pecculation* was substituted because it has a bit less larcenous sound, but they're all pretty unsavory.

Defeneration is only a little less disagreeable: "to exhaust by usury." Its neighbor *defenestration* seems innocuous enough, but since the act of throwing something out a window (L. *fenestra*) also included someone, or oneself, the word becomes a less attractive choice.

Vestal virgins found guilty of incontinence were subjected by the Romans to the peculiar and brutal punishment of live burial *(defossion),* certainly not high on the list of activities in which to involve oneself. *Decollation* (beheading) is unquestionably less inhumane but still undesirable.

The Latin *osculum* describes a "little mouth," or what you do with yours before you kiss, its second meaning. *Deosculation* means involvement in an affectionate kiss, a preferable and pleasurable activity for almost anybody.

What do these words have in common?

accommodate
affidavit
diphtheria
embarrass
inoculate
precede
siege
harass

These are the most commonly misspelled words in print. Only three of 172 schoolteachers could spell them all correctly. Here is a list of spellings that editors cannot agree upon:

taboo/tabu
adviser/advisor
traveler/traveller
bazaar/bazar
caffeine/caffein

G*ladstone, gallipot, tureen,* and *solander* are all

footwear
varieties of frogs
political terms
containers
items of cookery

William Ewart Gladstone (1809–1898) sustained enough popularity as British prime minister to have his name attached to several items. As Chancellor of the Exchequer, he lowered the English price on French wines by cutting the import duty, so that for a time inexpensive claret was called *Gladstone.* But by the end of the Victorian period, this term was forgotten—as was the convertible brougham that once bore his name—and the eponymic *Gladstone* lived on only as a name for the suitcase he frequently carried, a piece of hand luggage with two hinged compartments.

Occasionally in definition the simplest explanation is the accurate one (e.g., *plainsong* is "simple melody"), for a *gallipot* is no more than *galley + pot,* a small earthenware jar once used for medicines and imported from the Mediterranean by galleys.

Among historical French military figures only Napoleon distinguished himself more than the Vicomte de Turenne, marshal general of France in 1660. On one occasion this worthy innovator found himself at dinner with no bowl from which to serve the soup, and for the job he utilized his upturned helmet, the archetypal dinner dish that still bears his name.

Last on this list of containers is the *solander,* a book-shaped box to protect books, maps, or botanical specimens. Named after the Swedish botanist who devised it, Daniel C. Solander, the box may either be hinged or have two parts, one sliding into the other.

How are the *Thames* (river) and *platha* associated with the phrase "the King's English"?

Was the river name *Thames* ever pronounced with the *h,* to rhyme with *shames?* Yes, indeed, right up until 1714, the year that the House of Hanover began occupying the British throne. The first of these German monarchs was George I, who spoke only German, a language not famous for *th-* sounds, so that to George the river that coursed beside his palace was "de Temz." Since English spoken as it should be is "the King's (or Queen's) English," the implication being that the monarch is never wrong, thenceforth all British subjects and all who followed them pronounced *Thames* as it is said today.

In a portion of Spain the square in the center of town is called the *platha* because one long-forgotten, tongue-tied king could come no closer to *plaza* than that.

"Before escorting her to his bedroom, he put out the light, the cat, his cigar, and any further thoughts of celibacy." Within this irreverent quotation is a good example of a

zarf
zaguan
Zeitgeist
zori
zeugma

When the English language possesses no single-word equivalent for a foreign name or idea, it often simply adopts the word intact from the other language. No better examples of this borrowing can be found than among words beginning with *z.*

You may have held a chalice-like *zarf* in your hand today, the little plastic gizmo to hold those awful cone-shaped coffee cups that they have at art receptions and city council meetings. The dentist has a metal zarf for his patients' paper rinse cup, which is even worse. The word was borrowed unaltered from the Arabic language.

Old Spanish contributed *zaguan,* the little man-sized door within a larger door or gate designed so that a person can pass through without going to the trouble of opening the big gate. Occasionally, the word *postern* is inappropriately used for a door-within-a-door, but *postern* really just means a small rear gate, as in a fort or castle. The absence of an accurate English counterpart again promoted the adoption of the European word.

Certainly more than one word is necessary to define *Zeitgeist,* so the German term is appropriated: "the general intellectual, moral, and cultural level of an era; the spirit of the time, the social climate of the age; the taste and outlook characteristic of a period or generation."

I couldn't find a better word than *zori* for the sandal that's fastened to the foot by a thong passing between the big toe and the second toe—a benchmark of the simple Japanese style. It's their word for their article, just as *ziti* is Italian for that particular variety of macaroni.

A *zeugma* (Greek) is the rhetorical figure used by the speaker of the sentence quoted, in which his verb phrase *(put out)* is used to modify or govern two or more words *(light, cat, cigar,* and *thoughts),* although its use is logical only with one at a time: "She opened her heart and her pocketbook to the orphaned child."

Incidentally, did you notice how the speaker used *celibacy?*

Celibate is often thought to designate only one who is sexually continent, when historically it means simply "unmarried."

What do these words have in common?

nomenclature
homonym
onomastics
nom de plume
onomatopoeia

> What's in a name? that which we call a rose
> By any other name would smell as sweet.

Do you believe Juliet? Would a rose still have its sentimental charm and romantic image if it were called a *glitchblossom* or a *dungbutton*? Of course it wouldn't. Names are of paramount importance, and Juliet herself knew that a Capulet in love with a Montague would make her life and love vastly different than it would have been if she and Romeo had been from other families.

That even Shakespeare didn't believe it is illustrated again and again by the bard himself. Here's an example in *onomastics* (the study of naming) from the same playwright who once said it didn't matter what you named things. In a later play he invents another character, a wicked woman of savage nature and animal lusts, whose illicit passion for the bastard Edmund causes three deaths. Shakespeare casts about for a name for this villainess and forms a new word (he was responsible for some 1,700 neologisms) from the root for things sexual (Gk. *gono-*), so Goneril's name becomes a tag for her character. King Lear's good daughter, by contrast, is named *Cordelia* (L. *cor*, heart, as in *cordial* and *accordant*), a tag with a wholesome flavor.

In biblical times the importance of naming was explicit: naming a thing gave you power over it, and knowing a man's name somehow gave you a sort of hold over him. Genesis tells how Adam's naming of the beasts made him master of them all. The power over a man by knowing his name is no better illustrated than in the conversation between Moses and the burning bush. When Moses hears the voice from the bush assign him a dangerous rescue mission, he quite logically inquires, "Who shall I say sent me, what is your name?" With obvious respect for the ancient orthodoxy, the voice from the flames answers, *Yahweh.* ("I am who I am").

What's in a name? Everything.

M ark the one word that does not fit in with the other words:

  murphied
  mesmerized
  bliveted
  burked
  bowdlerized
  boycotted

A nubile woman who appears to be considerably younger than her years teams up with a husky older man of quiet dignity but forceful mien. Singly they infiltrate a rowdy Elks Club convention, where out-of-town revelers are on the prowl for a good time. From the pack the young woman cuts out Joe, well known among his friends as a party-boy par excellence, and after two drinks and half an hour's dalliance, she takes him upstairs to her hotel room.

Then at the most compromising of moments the well-built confederate lets himself into the room with his own key. Within the outraged harangue that follows, Joe learns that the confederate is in fact the girl's father. She is grossly underage, he is told, and Joe is guilty not just of an indiscretion but of statutory rape. When the confrontation calms down a bit, the "father" intimates that for a certain sum the matter might be forgotten.

At work two weeks later the sadder-but-wiser Joe ruefully tells his tale to a fellow employee, who shakes his head and says, "Poor Joe. You've been *murphied.*"

Were the original figures in this confidence game called Murphy, or was the title for the ploy somehow suggested by the bed of that name? Nobody knows; just the handy and specific verb remains.

The surname of Franz Anton Mesmer (1734–1815) became a verb under circumstances only a little less undignified, for this forerunner of Freud honestly believed in his power to cure emotional ills by what he termed "animal magnetism." Although Mesmer was knowledgeable in many fields, including medicine, he nevertheless became passionately immersed in the notion that the stars influence a cloud of magnetism that surrounds the universe. He devised a treatment in which his excited and spellbound patients reached a sort of emotional crisis that could be dispelled with a wave from his magnetic wand.

Though he cured many sufferers, Mesmer was forced to move from Vienna to Paris in 1778. Here, with the help of mood music and a tank of sulphuric acid, he was able to induce a hypnotic state which often ended with patients twitching and screaming. When the performances grew notorious enough to gain royal attention, Louis XVI appointed an investigative committee that included Benjamin Franklin and Antoine Lavoisier. They opined that the magnetic treatment methods were worthless, and the exiled Mesmer died later in Switzerland, unaware that he had pioneered the use of hypnotism in medicine—or that he had left behind his name as a synonym for *hypnotize.*

William Burke proved to be an entirely different sort of man from the prescient Doctor Mesmer. This Irish laborer was helping to dig the Scottish Union Canal in 1827 when an elderly fellow boarder died unexpectedly. When no relatives came forward to claim the body, Burke sold it to Edinburgh anatomist Robert Knox for 7s. 6d., a goodly sum in those days.

Human dissection enjoyed no public sanction at that time (illustrated by the clandestine grave robbery in *Tom Sawyer*), and fresh cadavers—particularly those undamaged by violent death*—were thus a marketable commodity. Burke recognized a potentially profitable sideline despite the attendant risks, and within a short time an alcoholic beggar woman disappeared from the streets of Edinburgh.

Teamed with his landlord and their two wives, Burke completed a grisly foursome that lured in hapless travelers, made them drunk, and furnished the dissection tables of the local medical school with suitable material. This gruesome tale ended with the smothering of one Mary Petersen, an eighteen-year-old woman of the streets who had been on intimate terms with some of the anatomy students to whom her body was assigned. This burst the bubble, and when the ringleader was led to the gallows, spectators shouted, "Burk him, burk him!"†

**Burk,* v., to kill by suffocation.
†Burke's final irony was to be dissected at a public lecture-demonstration.

"To expurgate prudishly" was shortened to a single-word verb when Thomas Bowdler, M.D. (fl. 1818) undertook to edit from Shakespeare those passages he regarded as indecent, so that the poet might "with propriety be read aloud in front of the family." By 1836, when Bowdler had cleaned up Gibbon's *History of the Decline and Fall of the Roman Empire, bowdlerize* came to mean any form of censorship perpetrated in the name of moral purity.

Rosie Boycott, great-great-niece of the famous Captain Charles Boycott, tells in her *Batty, Bloomers and Boycott/A Little Etymology of Eponymous Words* how her Irish ancestor was ostracized by his tenants for refusing to lower their rent after two years of bad potato crops. She writes that a local priest substituted *boycott* for *ostracize,* explaining that the peasantry would understand it better.

My retired army friend stoutly maintains that a *blivet,* the only non-eponymous word on the list, is two pounds of manure in a one-pound bag, but the broader definition is any useless contraption, like water wings for a fish or toothbrushes for chickens. Nobody seems to know its origin.

William F. Cody was NOT

alive during World War I
a buffalo soldier
a plainsman and scout
the owner of a wild west show
an Iowan

William Frederick ("Buffalo Bill") Cody, 1846–1917, was a native Iowan who worked as a plainsman and scout until 1883, when he opened his popular Buffalo Bill's Wild West Show, with which he toured many years. What Cody was not was a *buffalo soldier,* the phrase that designates a Negro military man. The name is said to have come from the American Indians, who did not scalp the black soldiers they killed in battle, allegedly because their hair was thought to resemble the buffalo's, an animal which furnished the Plains Indians most of their food and clothing.

What do these words have in common?

tantalizing
Sisyphean
Icarian
Delphic

Tantalus, Lydian king of Greek mythology, inspired in modern English both a verb and a noun. When he tested the gods' friendship once too often, Tantalus was punished with endless hunger and thirst. The banks of the lake in which he was imprisoned were overhung with luscious fruit just out of his reach, while the water about him receded each time he attempted to drink it—the epitome of a *tantalizing* situation. The gadget in which brandy decanters are locked (but in full sight) is appropriately called a *tantalus.*

The fate of Sisyphus, King of Corinth, proved every bit as maddening. For his greed Zeus sent him to Hades to try forever to roll a giant rock up a hill, down which it forever rolled again. A *Sisyphean* task never ends.

Icarian became synonymous with "perilously inadequate" when Icarus escaped from Crete's maze by flying out on wings designed by his father Daedalus.* But the wings were applied to his body with wax, which melted when he flew near the sun, and he fell from the sky and perished.

No less unhappy was the Greek warrior who sought advice from the Oracles at *Delphi,* the last of these four words of classical origin. When the warrior was given the unpunctuated sentence THOU SHALT GO THOU SHALT RETURN NEVER BY WAR SHALT THOU PERISH, he optimistically chose to put a period before *never,* instead of after it. He may or may not have realized, just before dying in battle, that the unpunctuated sentence was ambiguous, or *Delphic.*

What two similarities do these words share?

cardigan
balaclava
raglan
nightingale

Wars have always brought new words into the language. Each of these four items of apparel received its name from a place or a person taking part in the Crimean War (1853–1856). James Thompson Brudenell, Seventh Earl of Cardigan, figured in the "sweater war" as the leader of the Light Brigade in its famous and disastrous charge, which he happily survived. Lord Cardigan's name was applied to the jacket or sweater first worn in this conflict by the British troops.

---

*Daedalian, adj., intricate, cunningly formed.

The place charged upon by the ill-fated Light Brigade was named *Balaclava,* source of the name for the wool, one-piece combination cap and face cover worn by the soldiers there. A coat with sleeves not joined to the garment at the shoulder but sloping to the neck was first worn by Fitzroy Somerset, Lord Raglan, the commander-in-chief of the Crimean War. Though Raglan lost his right arm at Waterloo, his amputation seems not to have influenced the sleeve style that bears his name.

The "Lady of the Lamp" became famous during the Crimean War, organizing hospitals at Scutari and Balaclava against bitter opposition. Florence Nightingale quite incidentally contributed her name to a kind of flannel wrap used to cover the shoulders and arms of a bedridden patient.

Where does *booze* come from?

Many sources credit Colonel E. C. Booze, a Philadelphia distiller, for yet one more synonym for liquor and for drinking it.* In the early 1800s the colonel manufactured a bottle shaped like a miniature log cabin, with his name cast into its bottom.

In fact the verb *bousen* (Middle English, to carouse) is much older, so that *booze* as a verb probably preceded the noun. It is of interest that *booze* to an Englishman means beer and ale but not whisky, whereas the opposite seems to apply in the United States.

---

*In his delightful book *Words,* Paul Dickson lists 2,231 synonyms for *intoxicated,* swamping Benjamin Franklin's previous record of 228.

Bacchanalia, jeroboam, and *demijohn* all suggest

holiday spirits
holidays
spirits

Bacchanalia has undergone considerable linguistic pejoration. Originally Roman harvest festivals in honor of Bacchus, the god of wine, the bacchanalian ceremonies were at first held in secret and attended only by women. Later men were invited, and within a short time the Bacchanalia went the way of the Saturnalia, growing so rowdy and dissolute that the word became synonymous with drunken revelry, and the celebrations had to be banned.

The wine bottle called a *jeroboam* holds a generous 4/5 gallon and is humorously named for Jeroboam I, "mighty man of valor" (I Kings 28), but reputedly no stranger to bacchanalian vice. The old king would probably be only moderately put off to know his name was remembered thus, for the record shows that he "did sin, and . . . made Israel sin."

The name for the big liquor bottle encased in wickerwork is yet one more example of feckless Anglicization of French words, for *demijohn* has nothing to do with John or half of John; it was once *Dame Jeanne,* "Lady Jane."

Daguerreotype, silhouette, guillotine, and ampere have in common

    photographic functions
    national origins
    use as weaponry
    artistic sources
    electronic technology

Louis Daguerre made a place for himself in the history of photography when he shortened exposure time from eight hours to a startling twenty minutes. A painter of seventy-foot canvases, Daguerre was using the camera obscura when he became interested in recording a scene "by the spontaneous action of light." His silvered sheets of copper, developed with quicksilver and fixed with sodium thiosulfate, became the *daguerreotype*.

Stone Age portraitists tracing a back-lighted subject did it first, but their art form had to wait until the eighteenth-century for a title. Whether the name was furnished by the habit or hobby of eponymous Étienne de Silhouette is not certain. The habits of this notably stingy French comptroller were famous enough that by 1759 *à la Silhouette* equaled the British "on the cheap." Though his hobby was making this sort of picture, Silhouette's name is said by some to have been used merely because this is the least expensive way to make a picture.

Sitting with Benjamin Franklin and Antoine Lavoisier on the investigating committee that condemned Mesmer and mesmerism was Dr. Joseph Guillotin. A French physician who designed medical instruments—but not the execution device—

Guillotin proposed that the use of the *louisette* (introduced to France by Dr. Antoine Louis) be extended to all executions. Before his new policy was adopted, this relatively humane execution device was used only for the royalty and the politically elite. Aghast when his surname was later substituted for *louisette*—and even more so when the Reign of Terror saw so many of his countrymen beheaded—Guillotin disavowed the connotation with his name, but the new eponym stuck, and the original *louisette* is now forgotten.

The fourth and last of the quartet of eponymous Frenchmen in question is André Ampère, the brilliant mathematician and professor who defined a unit of electrical energy: one *ampere* is the unit of current that one *volt* (after Alessandro Volta) can send through one *ohm* (after George Ohm).

Albert, *wellington, derby, mackintosh,* and *bowler* are all

> nouns
> Britishers
> wearing apparel
> eponyms

Surely Queen Victoria and her era gave rise to as many new words as Shakespeare and the Elizabethans. Her consort Albert once received from a Birmingham jeweler a watch chain worn all the way across his vest, pocket to pocket. Prince Albert wore it (the chain, not the coat or the potato or the tobacco, though they're all *alberts,* too) so often that this particular piece of jewelry became known by his name. Victoria's son Edward was too portly to fasten the bottom button of his vest. When he simply left it unbuttoned, his subjects followed suit, and to this day all the men of the Western world, fat or thin, leave the last button on their vests undone.

Arthur Wellesley, First Duke of Wellington and perhaps the most famous of all England's soldiers, gave his name to an RAF bomber of World War II, a beef dish, a variety of fir tree, and numerous place names in both Great Britain and America. His name is of course best remembered for the *Wellington* boot, originally knee-high in front and cut away behind. Nowadays the British "wellies" are rubber boots of much less dashing style, but their name still comes from the Iron Duke himself.

Though of lesser title, Edward Stanley, Twelfth Earl of Derby, nevertheless begat two common nouns. The first is a particular style of stiff felt hat, and the second is the name for the annual stakes race held each June at Epsom Downs in England.

The Scottish chemist Charles Macintosh (1766–1843) invented and patented the formula for the kind of rubberized cloth used to make the raincoat that bears his name. The word became so firmly identified with waterproof rainwear that a *mac* finally came to mean any sort of raincoat at all.

The *bowler* was popular enough that it acquired its lower-case distinction quickly.* John Bowler manufactured hats rather than designed them, and his product is so common in some places that it seems almost like a uniform.

---

*Loss of its capitalization is an ironic but accurate index of the success of an eponym; *Sandwich, Tuxedo, Saxophone,* and *Pasteurization* nowadays look a bit out of place capitalized.

The word *bogart,* used as a verb, would most likely be recognized by a member of

the Hollywood Society of Producers
and Directors
a graduate of the Lauren Bacall School
of Method Acting
the drug culture
the jet set
the Mafia

Willard Espy records *Mafia* as an acronym ("*M*orte *A*i *F*rancesi gl'*I*taliani *A*nelo," a thirteenth-century Sicilian battle cry), but points out that *Brewer's* says it's an Arabic word for "place of refuge." In any case the members of the Mafia or the jet set are not invariably up on the terminology of the drug culture, who claim the verb *bogart*.

It's hard to imagine a picture of ole Bogey without his cigarette dangling from his slack lip, but the verb born from his surname pertains to the smoking of marijuana rather than tobacco. The smoker who bogarts a joint holds it in his mouth longer than etiquette allows before he passes it on to his neighbor.

Fill in the blanks with the figures of speech from the list below that describe the italicized words in the paragraph.

_____	In 1987 the players of the NFL announced they were planning a strike with all *deliberate speed.*
_____	This news raised the *fackles of the hans,* and
_____	*the League said* that patience and perseverance
_____	would be necessary, that *hopefully* order would
_____	be maintained. An *assembled gathering* in New York featured members from the manage-
_____	ment *laying down their swords* and vowing to be
_____	*peaceful as doves.* A prominent player leaped to the podium and paraphrased, *"We came, we*
_____	*saw, we conquered,"* and then said gravely, "This
_____	is *not an inauspicious occasion."* With that he
_____	left the meeting *in high spirits and a tan Cadillac.*

asyndeton	personification
litotes	simile
metonymy	solecism
zeugma	spoonerism
oxymoron	tautology

Whether or not the members of the Supreme Court intended to achieve epigrammatic effect with their 1954 rhetorical figure "with all deliberate speed," they have been often quoted, and their phrase has become a famous example of the *oxymoron.* Greek *oxy-* (sharp) + *morus* (foolish) is the conjunction of incongruous or contradictory terms like *sweet sorrow, mournful optimist,* and *natural makeup.* New oxymorons spring into print every day: at Ruidoso Downs in New Mexico a jockey's name is transliterated *Quiet Boo.* It says in today's newspaper that if you have fifty thousand dollars but not a hundred thousand, the bank will sell you a *minijumbo* certificate of deposit. My favorite oxymoron has always been *bittersweet.*

Here's a bit of poetic doggerel that's barren of art but rich in oxymorons:

Oxymoronic

New York is: An elite rabble
Multitudinously few,
A monoglottal babble
Anciently new.

London is: An oriental West End
Tonefully flabby
And penniless nabobs
Fashionably shabby.

Paris is: An Eiffel blindness
Of lifeless verve,
A savant mindless
Of unproduced oeuvre.

The funny interchange of first syllables or sounds of words— ostensibly accidental—like *fackles of the hans,* has in recent years been subjected to soberer scrutiny. The much-quoted William Archibald Spooner (1844–1930), dean of New College, Oxford, spoke so memorably of God ("Our Lord is a shoving leopard"), queen ("that queer old dean"), country ("When the boys come home, we'll have all the hags flung out"), and sports ("For pure enjoyment, give me a well-boiled icycle") that any such humorous inversion is called a *spoonerism.*

But the picture of the benignant and absent-minded professor who once preached on "Kinquering Congs" has clouded: in a 1977 presidential address before the Royal Society of Medicine,

John M. P. Potter reminded his listeners that even during Spooner's lifetime, colleagues* suspected a more extensive brain dysfunction. In addition to his peculiar speech characteristics (which neurologists call *dysphasia*), Spooner also exhibited in his writing "anticipation" (inserting words too early in sentences) and "perseveration" (repeating phrases unnecessarily). Evidence of cerebral derangement suggested by these writing lapses *(dysgraphia)*† is augmented by accounts of Spooner's reversals of not only words but actions: on one occasion he poured wine onto some salt he had accidentally spilled on the tablecloth, an inappropriate reversal *(dyspraxia)* of cleaning wine stains with salt.

So it is that the relentless investigations of medical historians—as in the case of "Ring Around the Rosy"—have darkened the reputation of yet another cherished rhetorical device. In a commentary on Potter's speech, Doctor Samuel Vaisrub suggests that Spooner's imitators might have been a bit more compunctious about their contributions if they had been "constrained by humane considerations not to laugh at a handicap or by fear of being branded as brain damaged themselves."‡ Maybe it's just as well; if these disclosures had come earlier, the world might have had to do without Ed Wynn's introduction of sailors in a Broadway musical: "I bred my cast upon the waters" and a hurried newscaster's "Good evening ladies and gentlemen of the audio radiance." In any case we'll always relish the originator's very own apology for his lack of musicality: "I know only two tunes—'God Save the Weasel' and 'Pop Goes the Queen.' "

---

*Notably Sir Julian Huxley.
†He helpfully left a diary of 250,000 words.
‡*Journal of the American Medical Association* 237(7):677, February 14, 1977.

A rhetorical figure in which inanimate objects (like the tippling ten-dollar bill in O. Henry's "The Tale of a Tainted Tenner") or abstractions ("Love walked right in . . .") are endowed with human qualities is called a *personification.* Of course, everybody understands that the writer means it's the representatives of the NFL, rather than the League itself, who issue statements and deny rumors. In this instance the metonymy and personification have been used so long that they are hardly noticed.

If the League representatives really said, *"Hopefully* order would be maintained," they very likely wanted to convey the sentiment "We hope order will be maintained," when in fact the grammatical meaning of their statement is "If/when order is maintained, it will be with hope." A recent usage panel declined 70–30 to accept this *solecism* (Gk. *soloikos,* speaking incorrectly, referring to the corrupt Attic dialect spoken by Athenians in Soloi), ubiquitous though it may be.

A *tautology* (Gk. *tauto,* the same + *logos,* word) describes needless repetition of the same sense in different words, redundancy. A *gathering* is by definition already *assembled.*

Members of that "gathered assembly" of course had no swords to lay down; the word *sword* is a metonymic designation of something like "violent opposition," *metonymy* being a figure of speech in which an idea (e.g., peace) is evoked by means of some associated notion (the laying down of swords).

A *simile* is the comparison of two things (in this case *peaceful* and *doves*), using the words *like* or *as.*

History's most famous *asyndeton* (Gk. *a-,* not + *syndetos,* bound together = *asyndeton,* without conjunctions) is Julius Caesar's *"Veni, vidi, vici"*—paraphrased by the speaker from the podium. The word *podium* is mistakenly used for *lectern* even by a good many people who spend a lot of time standing on them and who know that Greek *pous* means "foot."

An affirmative can be expressed by the negation of its opposite. Every ear hears important differences between "She's a beautiful woman" and "She's not an ugly woman," even though the sentences are similar. The speaker who negated the opposite in "This is not an inauspicious occasion" would have spoken more forcefully if he had avoided the *litotes.* Listen to its use by a master of rhetorical devices: "This is not the end. It is not even the beginning of the end. But it is, perhaps, the end of the beginning."*

Remember the seducer who put out the light, the cat, his cigar, and further thoughts of celibacy? Here the writer applies a yoke (Gk. *zeugma*) to two incongruous phrases *(high spirits and tan Cadillac)* governed by the same verb *(left).*

What were (originally) "the three R's"?

Like Bismarck's "blood and iron" speech and Churchill's "blood, sweat, and tears" acceptance oratory, "reading, 'riting, and 'rithmetic" is so catchy and appealing to the ear that the original quotation is almost forgotten. Bismarck really said, ". . . this [rescue of Germany] cannot be accomplished by speeches and resolutions of a majority, but only by iron and blood [*Eisen und Blut*]." Taking office as prime minister, Churchill offered only "blood, toil, tears, and sweat." The original "three R's" were "reading, reckoning, and rhetoric," a triad known to alarmingly few pedagogues.

---

*Winston Churchill, after the Battle of Egypt.

How is it that *infantry* doesn't mean "the trappings of infants" like *gallantry* means the trappings of gallants or *carpentry* the work of carpenters?

It is the acquisition of speech that makes a child of an *infant* (L. *in-*, not + *fans,* able to speak). The young boys who once took care of knights' equipment were not babies, but they were not of age and thus not permitted to speak for themselves. It was for this reason they were known in Italian as *infanteria,* the forerunner of our modern word for foot soldiers.

The best husband for whom a woman might wish would be

polygynous
edentulous
penurious
uxorious
philandering

Few women would seek a husband described as *polygynous* (Gk. *poly-,* many + *gynē,* woman, wife) or *polygamous* (*gamy,* marriage). One who had no teeth *(edentulous)* would be unquestionably less undesirable, yet still not among the upper echelon of suitors. A miserly and stingy *(penurious)* mate would be troublesome and tedious, and no woman wants that. What most women would like is for a man to be *uxorious,* excessively—even a little foolishly—fond of his wife (L. *uxor*).

How did a word that means "loving one's husband" (Gk. *philo-,* love + *andros,* man, husband) come to mean "engage in frivolous love affairs" *(philander)*? Nobody knows the first author who mistakenly adapted the name Philander from the Greek *philandros* (loving men, loving one's husband), but Philander became a traditional literary name for lover, from medieval romances to the Restoration. The word is a little like *philology* (Gk. *philo-*, love + *logos*, word), which ought to mean "word lover" but is the specialized term for historical linguistics.

Identify these occupations:

    scrimshander
    cooper
    luthier
    farrier
    navvy

The origin for the name of the artisan who produces scrimshaw work, *scrimshander,* is obscure, though the surname *Scrimshaw* suggests an eponym. This intricate and meticulous carving of ivory, bone, and shells—often highlighted with graphite—is said to have been a popular pastime among sailors during long whaling voyages.

The barrel maker derives his name from the German *Kupe* (cask, barrel), and *cooper* as a verb (to construct something from staves) is a common term in woodworking. In this instance, the surname Cooper probably evolved from the process, like *Tanner* and *Spicer* and *Tucker* (cloth-maker), rather than the other way around, like *macadam* and *vulcanize* and *scrimshander.*

At first the *luthier* made only wooden (Ar. *al-'ud,* the wood) lutes, the stringed instruments popular from the fourteenth to the seventeenth centuries, but now he also constructs guitars, violins, and other instruments as well.

Though nowadays horses are shod with aluminum as well as other metals, the *farrier* who does the job takes his occupational name from the Latin word for "iron," *ferrum,* the same root that produces *ferrule* (metal ring), *ferroconcrete* (reinforced masonry), and *ferriferous* (containing iron).

Some nineteenth-century English wag used *navigator* to describe the laborer who helped dig the British inland canal system. When the waterways were finished, this humorous term was shortened to *navvy* and applied to the unskilled laborer who now works on the streets. The Latin *navis* (ship) also figures in the word for the central part of a cathedral *(nave),* drawing from the metaphor of the church as a ship.

How would you rather be caught?

in flagrante delicto
in camera
in extremis
in omnia paratus

A hundred years ago travel to India was fraught with more peril than it is today. Travelers routinely dusted the locks of their suitcases with ninhydrin (commonly known as *nin*), a powerful protein dye that turns bright red on contact with the skin. Unwitting pilferers were thus literally caught red-handed, *in flagrante delicto,* in the very act of committing a crime.

It's annoying to be caught in private *(in camera)* and downright disastrous to be found at the brink of death *(in extremis)*. Indeed, if one must be caught at all, *in omnia paratus* (prepared for all things) would be easily the least objectionable condition, as any Boy Scout would affirm.

In what way are words like *tawdry, llama,* and *humble* opposite words like *auger, adder, apron,* and *orange*?

You have read the sad account of Saint Audrey of Ely and of how usage transferred the *t* from her title to her name to make *tawdry*. If the *llama* acquired his extra *l* by retrogressive assimilation, I cannot find it, for the South American ruminant mammal's scientific name is *Lama peruna*.

The phrase *to eat humble pie* has to do with neither humility nor dessert—though nowadays the speaker who says "I was forced to eat humble pie" intends to convey the sense of "I was humiliated." *Umbles* were once* the very cheapest cuts of meat—entrails—and those who were obliged to fill their pies with them were destitute rather than debased. Perhaps it was their very meanness that made them purloin the *h*.

In contrast to the words to which usage has added letters, the original forms of *auger, adder,* and *apron* have lost their initial letters. *A nauger* was once a tool just for piercing wheel hubs; now *an auger* drills holes in wood larger than those made by a gimlet, and it bores very large holes in the earth.

The venomous snake of Europe was once *a naddre,* rather than *an adder*—a bit more comprehensible deletion, when you consider the *a/an* articles, though it's not very clear why we

---

*Even earlier they were *numbles*.

haven't come to say "a nenvelope" and "a nelephant" by the same process.

The Latin *mappa* (napkin, towel) begat our present-day *napery,* the collective word for household linen, especially table linen. *Mop, nappe,* and *map* also descended from *mappa,* as did *apron,* which at one time was *napron.*

"Norange" should have traveled to English intact from the Sanskrit *nāraṅga* or the Hindi *nārangī,* east Indian words from the country where the fruit was first found. What happened to the initial *n?* Ask any linguist and you'll be told: "It's historical." Come to think of it, half the questions of the world might be answered that way.

E*sclavage, lavaliere, intaglio, chatelaine,* and *torque* are all

  light fixtures
  varieties of print
  items of jewelry
  mechanical principles

A language instructor once told me that lots of unfamiliar French nouns beginning with *é* could be roughly translated by mentally substituting an *s* (*école,* school; *étude,* study; *étrange,* strange). If there was already an *s,* he said, you could just delete the *e* (*estomac,* stomach; *esprit,* spirit; *espace,* space). The trick works moderately well for *esclavage* (slavery), a necklace made up of multiple rows of beads or jewels, so named from its resemblance to the fetters of a slave. The manacles worn on slaves' wrists yielded a term for the popular *slave bracelet.*

In the manner of Prince Albert and his watch chain, the

mistress of Louis XIV, Louise de La Vallière, gave her name to the *lavaliere,* a pendant worn on a chain around the neck.

Intaglio (from It. *intagliare,* to cut in, engrave) describes a method of engraving printing plates, but it's also the word for the gem or stone so incised, like a cameo. The pronunciation ignores the *g:* een-TAH-lyoh.

A *chatelain* was once the keeper of a castle (L. *castellum*), and his lady was the *chatelaine.* The clasp or chain worn at the waist originally held his keys and her purse; now, the name for the lady has become the term for this particular sort of jewelry.

Torque has a complicated mechanical definition, but in a broader sense it means "a turning or twisting force." Originally a strip of twisted metal worn by the ancient Gauls as a necklace or armband, now *torque* can refer to any necklace, of various materials, shaped by the technique of twisting.

C*aul, sibyl,* and *sortilege* all suggest

    deviation
    devolution
    divination
    divinities

In a novelistic detail auguring his character's eventual good fortune, Dickens has David Copperfield born in a *caul.* This fluid-filled membrane that encloses the unborn baby is occasionally intact at birth, covering the head like a cap (Fr. *cale*). Among other Victorian superstitions about such rare birth circumstances was the belief that a person so born could never drown. That property apparently being transferable, Copperfield's mother offered it for sale to a sailor, to forestall his occupational hazard. An old lady later won the caul in a raffle and found it effective, for she in fact did not drown but "died triumphantly in bed, at ninety-two." Folklore surrounding the caul is still alive and well in America. In Red River County, Texas, where I grew up, the heterodoxy was clear: they believed that such a baby would someday be able to foretell the future.

The story of the very first Sibylla is lost in antiquity, but it is clear she was a seeress and an oracle. By and by, *sibyl* became a title for any woman to whom Apollo granted the gift of prophecy—along with the number of years of life equal to the grains of sand she could hold on her palm—and in time, *sibylline* came to mean "prophetic, oracular, mysterious."

The practice of foretelling the future by drawing lots is called *sortilege* (L. *sors,* lot + *legere,* to read). Usage has broadened the word to include the practice of any sorcery or witchcraft. To "accept one's lot" in life, or to trust in "the luck of the draw" are more respectable adages that have grown out of this sort of divination.

The exclamation "Holy moly!" could be characterized as:

> a comment on the nature of a potion
> an allusion to classical mythology
> a candidate for the game of "Reduplication"
> a stinky pinky

The story of the herbal potion of Hermes just *has* to have some message for modern times. In the *Odyssey* Homer tells of

Circe, a beautiful and dangerous witch who turns men into swine. They grunt and root in her sty, eating the acorns she gives them, but inside they know they're still men, disgusted by their vile state, yet powerless under her charm. To protect Odysseus from this bestial spell, Hermes administers *moly,* the lily leek with yellow flowers and black roots. When Circe applies her magic, Odysseus does not change but remains a beautiful youth. Because he has resisted her enchantment, Circe falls in love with Odysseus and keeps him at her castle for a year's feasting. The *Odyssey* is like Genesis: it's a marvelous story to read, even if you don't believe in mythology.

In Joe Shipley's compendium of word games, *Playing with Words,* he reminds us how the ear relishes repetitious sounds, and he enumerates the four varieties of duplicated words for his game of "Reduplication": the two parts are identical *(pawpaw, jubjub);* the initial consonant changes *(hodgepodge, hurdy-gurdy);* the vowel changes *(wishy-washy, riffraff);* or both change *(linsey-woolsey, pish-tush).* He observes how the Yiddish sound *sch-* * is used with derision but vigor as a duplication of denigration, as in *husband-schmusband* or *working-schmirking.*

Where I live the game is called "Stinky Pinky," and the combination is usually a noun with one rhyming adjective. One player gives the definition—sometimes with a hint—and the others try to guess the stinky pinky:

Q: Somebody who stares at electromagnetic energy beams.
     (Hint: It's a "stink*er* pink*er.* ")
A: A laser gazer.

---

*Unfailingly distasteful, as in *schmo, schnook, schnorrer, schlock, schlemiel.*

Q: A possum's trademark. (It's a "stink*o* pink*o*.")
A: A Pogo logo.

Q: A sacred lily leek. (It's a "stink*y* pink*y*.")
A: Holy moly!

And so on.

Match the gift with its recipient:

GIFT	RECIPIENT
lagniappe	carnival-goer
oblation	*poule*
sop	Episcopal Church
kickback	sommelier
gratuity	graduation speaker
cumshaw	grocery store customer
sportula	Cerberus
handsel	racketeer
solatium	Hong Kong tour guide
fairing	needy family
honorarium	business partner
un petit cadeau	injured party in a lawsuit

When the English language lacks an exact word for a practice, a foreign term is often adopted intact. For example, in the good old days before cash-and-carry supermarkets, the credit grocer gave his customer a little present—like a carton of Cokes—at the time he paid his monthly bill. Louisianans heard their Cajuns* call the gift a *lagniappe* and assimilated the spe-

---

*Who got it from American Spanish *la ñapa*, "the addition."

cific word into English; similarly, Southwestern Americans borrowed *pilon* from Spanish to designate the same gift.

The Episcopal Church is the recipient of an *oblation* (L. *oblatus,* one offered to God). Capitalized, the word denotes the bread and wine of the Eucharist itself.

A sibyl of ancient Greek myth was conducting Aeneas on a tour through Hades. When she found its door guarded by a vicious three-headed dog named Cerberus, she threw him a sop of poppies (opium) and honey that promptly put him to sleep. Accordingly, a *sop* became any bribe to quiet a troublesome person. A bit of soggy bread isn't worth much, and this implication persists with modern usage; a *sop* is of little more than token value.

Of course the *racketeer* gets the *kickback,* and the wine steward *(sommelier)* pockets the *gratuity.*

Pidgin English fashioned *cumshaw* from Amoy *kam sia,* the island dialect for the Mandarin Chinese *kan hsieh* (*kan,* to feel + *hsieh,* gratitude), an appropriate sentiment for a tourist who's just been guided through Hong Kong.

The *needy family* who is given a basket of food at Christmas has received a *sportula,* the unaltered Latin word for "little basket," while on New Year's Day business partners exchange *handsels* as tokens of mutual esteem.

From the same Latin word that provides *solace* comes *solatium,* a gift of compensation for damage to the feelings as distinct from financial loss or physical suffering—not an uncommon request in a civil lawsuit.

The carnival-goer who is given the Kewpie doll (that seldom really looks like Cupid) for knocking down all the milk bottles with a baseball has received a *fairing.* The professional person who speaks at a graduation ceremony is rewarded with an *honorarium,* "a gift not legally owed."

In a Southwestern city, far removed from things Gallic, I recently saw a new shop called *Un Petit Cadeau.* An appropriate enough title, at least by the literal translation, but I couldn't decide whether the owner who named his shop "A Little Gift" was ignorant of French idiom or poking a bit of fun at his unwitting customers. The French *poule* ("chicken," literally, but extended to mean "lady of the night") receives *un petit cadeau* in return for her services. Though I was in a hurry at the time, I wanted to go into the shop to see what sort of goods were for sale. I didn't stop, and I've regretted it ever since.

Zuzu, gedunk, and *pogey bait* are all

    items of fishing tackle
    nongourmet foods
    espionage words
    unintelligent or doltish persons
    racial slur words

In current Black English a *zuzu* is anything to eat that is wrapped in cellophane and bought from a vending machine. The archetypal Zuzu was a patented gingersnap baked and sold by Nabisco as late as 1916. Just like any popular eponym, the brand name comes into its own when it loses its capitalization and broadens itself into a generic term. *Aspirin, cellophane, nylon,* and *moxie* (originally a soft drink) once were specific brand names, as is *Scotch tape.* Not surprisingly, it's the trade names made into verbs that arrive most vigorously: *Xerox* seems to have been around forever, and *Sanforize* is well on its way.

The generic word for junk food in the U.S. Navy is *gedunk,* where a snack cart or food trolley is often called a *gedunk wagon.* I saw it spelled *g'dong* once, and then *gedong,* and it was from this last variant spelling that I found its origin: *gedong* is one spelling of the Anglo-Indian *godown,* "a place where goods are kept." Perhaps it was some nameless naval officer just returning from India who named the wagon from which snack foods were sold.

Also of military origins and clouded etymology is *pogey bait,* candy or sweets used as gifts to a woman in return for sexual favors. That *pogey* is also one term for a homosexual suggests that it might be a word for that sort of inducement as well, and this has been corroborated by veterans of the 1940s and 1950s. To confuse the etymology further, a *poggie* is an army recruit, and *pogey* can mean both "poorhouse, workhouse, or government custodial institution" and the food served in such a place.

Name the author responsible for these three adjectives:

Pecksniffian
Micawberish
Pickwickian

Language can pay no greater tribute to a novelist than to make adjectives from his characters' names. Once again, the phenomenon of a name's becoming a common descriptive word is analogous to the lowercased eponym or the broadened trade name. *Dickensian* itself describes a particular literary style, and it is Charles Dickens whose indelible characters brought these three adjectives into the language. From Seth Pecksniff, the obsequious architect in *Martin Chuzzlewit* (1843), *Pecksniffian* has come to describe the hypocrite who insincerely affects goodwill or lofty morality.

Mr. Wilkins Micawber provided David Copperfield with endless projections of bubble schemes sure to lead to great fortunes. Though his pie-in-the-sky propositions never worked out, Micawber remained optimistic, certain that something would turn up. Some scholars think that Dickens modeled this character after his own father; in any case his depiction proved vivid enough to make *Micawberish* the adjective for a confident but thriftless idler who is always sure something will turn up.

Dickens' meticulous description of the fat boy in *The Posthumous Papers of the Pickwick Club* (1836) was accurate enough for doctors to diagnose him a hundred years later—only after medical technology had advanced far enough. Marked obesity combined with inactivity can stifle respiration enough to allow blood carbon dioxide to rise. Every time Dickens' fat boy sat down, he went to sleep. Today this physiological phenomenon is called the Pickwick Syndrome, and its sufferers are described as *Pickwickian.*

Charles Dickens' prototypical creations fill many a thesis and dissertation. A *Little Nell* (from *The Old Curiosity Shop,* 1840) can be any saccharine, cloying heroine, as surely as a *Scrooge* (from *A Christmas Carol,* 1843) is the quintessential skinflint; *Fagin* (from *Oliver Twist,* 1837) personifies all fawning villains, and any character who belabors the obvious is recognized as a *Gradgrind* (found in *Hard Times,* 1845).

The most helpful item at an exhumation would be a

bilduke
duke's mixture
folie à deux
deus ex machina

Anyone assigned the unwelcome duty of exhuming or digging up a body (L. *ex-,* out + *humus,* earth) would look about for a shovel. Though an occasional lexicographer assigns an apocryphal Bill Duke as eponymous, *bilduke* probably comes from the older *belduque,* a narrow shovel or sharpshooter.

Duke's mixture is one of the many phrases for "assortment." Unless, however, the assortment was one of various kinds of earth-moving equipment, it would be of little use at an exhumation.

The two sisters in *Arsenic and Old Lace* pose a fine theatrical illustration of *folie à deux* (madness for two), identical manifestations of insanity affecting two individuals, usually two members of the same family living together. The addition of their bewildered and hallucinatory brother might make it *folie à trois.*

A Greek dramatist whose plot became too bogged down for resolution in the final act devised a novel solution. When his convoluted story grew unmanageably complex and too involved for explanation within the alloted time, the playwright mechanically lowered a box (Gk. *mēchanē,* L. *machina*) onto the stage. A god (L. *deus*) stepped out and explained to the audience what finally happened to the actors and situations.

Though this sort of finale would very likely fail on Broadway, the Greek audiences evidently didn't mind. From this histrionic gimmick comes the phrase *deux ex machina,* an artificial or improbable device used to resolve the difficulties of a plot. In certain cases a *deus ex machina* is a person who unexpectedly intervenes to resolve a situation.

Which of these would be the least objectionable answer to a problem?

a Pyrrhic victory
a draconian resolution
a procrustean solution
a Promethean action

In 279 B.C. Pyrrhus, King of Epirus, assembled a huge army, complete with elephants, and defeated the Romans at Asculum. But his casualties were so heavy that he reportedly commented, "One more such victory and I am lost." This rueful admission brought *Pyrrhic victory* into the language, a victory won with staggering losses, a fairly objectionable answer to any problem.

Draco earned his infamous reputation in ancient Athens by devising laws of such extreme severity that his name became synonymous with harshness. A *draconian resolution* would by its very inclemency be objectionable.

Greek mythology rather than Greek history supplies Procrustes, a vicious highwayman who seized travelers and either stretched or shortened them to fit his iron bed. A *procrustean solution* is out of the question.

Prometheus is from the same literature, but where Procrustes' story is barbaric, Prometheus' is illustrious. Along with the taming of horses and the concoction of medicine, this resourceful Titan gave the earth one of its most precious possessions, fire (which he stole from heaven). *Promethean* implies "boldly creative, life-bringing"—a fine way to solve a problem.

The antonyms *gargantuan* and *lilliputian* have come from the works of two writers less dissimilar than their adjectives. Name the books and their authors.

In Rabelais' satire *Gargantua and Pantagruel,* the giant from the medieval fabliau is born from his mother's left ear (shouting "Drink, drink, drink!") and engages in such buffooneries as combing cannonballs from his hair and stealing the bells of Notre Dame Cathedral to hang around his horse's neck. From this Renaissance satire the adjective *gargantuan* has come to describe anything of immense size or volume, from the giant ape in the movies to the amount of water in Halley's Comet.

Jonathan Swift's satirical *Gulliver's Travels* also employs stature as a metaphor for human attributes, but the pettiness of Lilliputian life (and that of eighteenth-century England, Swift implies) is emphasized by their size: one-twelfth of normal. Thus *lilliputian* as an adjective means not only "diminutive" but "trivial, petty."

Where would you rather be?

in a columbarium
on a cenotaph
in an encomium
on a catafalque

It is with some evidence of disregard for bird names that a dove (L. *columba*) lives in a *pigeonhole* of a dovecote or *columbarium,* but it's clear enough that the "vault with niches for urns containing ashes of the dead" resembled the dovecote enough to share its name. Since you must be dead and reduced to ashes to be placed in a columbarium, it's likely a place you'd rather not be.

In a similar sepulchral vein a *cenotaph* (Gk. *kenos,* empty + *taphos,* tomb) is a monument erected in the name of a dead person whose remains lie somewhere else. The raised structure upon which a coffin rests during a state funeral is called a *catafalque* (It., from *cata,* down from + *fala,* scaffold), last in this funerary triad.

It's true that an *encomium* might be offered as a eulogy, but the original Greek *enkomion* was a "speech in praise of a conqueror," and the modern encomium most commonly retains that meaning: "a formal expression of lofty praise and tribute." An encomium is an agreeable—even enviable—place in which to find oneself.

A small metal box on a doorpost containing quotations from Deuteronomy is called a

meshuggah
mezuzah
megillah
mazuma
mamzer

Stating the law of Moses for a second time, Deuteronomy (Gk. *deuter,* second + *nomos,* law) includes

> And thou shalt love the Lord thy God with all thine heart, and with all thy soul, and with all thy might. . . .
> And thou shalt write them upon the posts of thy house, and on thy gates.

Four thousand years later faithful members of this religion still enclose this quotation within a metal box called a *mezuzah* (Hebrew, doorpost) and fasten it to the doorposts of their houses.

Some of the liveliest and most vigorous additions to contemporary English are words borrowed from Hebrew and Yiddish, the latter a blend of High German and Hebrew. *Audacity* and *chutzpah* (pronounced HUTZ-pah) are pretty much the same things, but almost everybody would rather be described with the Yiddishism.

Meshuggah (muh-SHOO-guh) means "crazy, insane," and the word both looks and sounds like it. The Yiddish slang for money *(mazuma)* is a little like the American slang *spondulicks:* somehow the very word you use for cash suggests the nature of what's to be bought with it. *Simoleons* just *must* be spent for something frivolous. Who could buy a C.D. with *smackers?*

A child born of a marriage forbidden by the Jewish faith is a *mamzer* (MAHM-zuh), but slang has further particularized the word to make it synonymous with *bastard. Megillah* (muh-GIL-uh) has been similarly expanded by usage; originally a scroll containing portions of Jewish Scripture, a megillah now can be any tedious and overlong account, a shaggy dog story.

M atch the word from the list on the left with its synonym from the list on the right:

flirt	unbeliever
bridal	painted red
tuxedo	throw flowers
amazon	carousal
miniature	flat-chested
Galilean	wolf

Suggested origins of *flirt* evidently assume amalgamation of French *fleurette* (little flower) and early French *fleureter* (to use flowery language) to the Anglo-Saxon *flurt* (to throw rapidly or jerkily).

Those who gave wedding parties in old England served nothing more elegant than beer—ostensibly well received, for *bride's ale* (which became *bridale* and finally *bridal*) became the name of the party itself. German guests whose tankards were *gar aus* (empty) often were inclined to do just that: *carouse.*

Like other items of clothing, *tuxedo* took its name from its place of origin,* Tuxedo Park, New York, where that evening garment was first worn. *Tuxedo* as the place name began as an American Indian name for "wolf."

A story from Greek mythology is said to have been made up just to make room for the word *amazon.* These fierce female soldiers from Scythia were said to have cut off their right breasts to facilitate their archery (Gk. *a,* without + *mazos,* breast). The South American river got its name from the Spanish explorer Orellana, who fought tribes of women warriors he found along it and remembered the Greek tale.

Those painstaking painters who illuminated medieval manuscripts were called *miniators* (L. *minium*, red lead) from their use of cinnabar. Relatively narrow margins dictated smaller art work, but the color—rather than the size—gave us *miniature,* a small painting executed with great detail.

That *Galilean* once meant "unbeliever" is indeed ironic. But the Hebrew phrase that produced the name *Galilee* is *galil hagoyim,* "the place of the *goyim* (unbelievers)."

W rite the shorter word derived from each of these:

milliarium ⎯⎯⎯⎯⎯
chrysanthemum ⎯⎯⎯⎯⎯
Tutankhamen ⎯⎯⎯⎯⎯
jinriksha ⎯⎯⎯⎯⎯
budgerigar ⎯⎯⎯⎯⎯

Typically filled with the Roman passion for measurement and order, first emperor Augustus had his slaves set up a stone

---

*Like *jeans* (*Genes,* Genoa), *suede* (Sweden), and *cashmere* (Kashmir); as well as *jersey, challis,* and *fustian.*

in the center of the Forum. From this *milliarium* all distances were to be reckoned. Each thousand *(mille)* paces (equal to two steps or five feet) in every direction was marked by a milestone, complete with Augustus' name carved on it, of course. These measurements brought us the English *mile* of 5,280 feet.

The gold (Gk. *chrysos*) flower (Gk. *anthemon*) is shortened to *mum* possibly for the same reason *King Tutankhamen* shrank to *Tut:* the words offer some difficulty in spelling. It isn't nearly so clear why *rickshaw* has supplanted the straightforward *jinriksha:* Japanese *jin,* "man" + *rik,* "power" + *sha,* "vehicle."

The native Australian word *budgerigar* seems as though it ought to be an onomatopoeia, but it is not: *budgeri,* "good" + *gar,* "cockatoo." The difficult pronunciation for this name for an Australian parakeet has attenuated it to *budgie.*

Match each word on the left with its antonym from the list at the right:

haw	persona grata
cosmos	fruitful
au fond	gee
bête noire	chaos
bootless	torpor
brio	superficially

The origins of *gee* and *haw* as commands to a horse or ox to turn right or left, respectively, are unknown, though it is likely the words were chosen for their very difference in pronunciation—just as *k* and *w* are most often used in radio call letters because their sounds are seldom confused with other letters.

The universe regarded as an orderly, harmonious whole is the *cosmos* (Gk. *kosmos,* order), harmony and order as distinct from *chaos,* total disorder or confusion (Gk. *chaos,* empty space).

The French phrase *au fond* (oh-FÕ, at bottom) means "basically, thoroughly," and thus the opposite of *superficially.* The same language is also responsible for *bête noire* (black beast), indicating someone or something that one finds especially disagreeable or unacceptable. From the patois of diplomacy comes *persona grata,* "an acceptable person," especially a diplomat who is fully acceptable to a foreign government.

Vestiges of the archaic verb *to boot* (to be of help or advantage) remain in the regional English noun *boot,* "something given in addition, as a bonus in a swap or sale." Its negative as a synonym for *fruitless* has been alive and well at least since Shakespeare's time:

> When in disgrace with fortune and men's eyes,
> I all alone beweep my outcast state`
> And trouble deaf heaven with my *bootless* cries . . .
>
> Sonnet 29

Italians borrowed *brio* (vigor, vivacity) from Gaulish *brigo-* (strength, might) for notations on their musical scores, and rhymesters have borrowed it from them. (All good limericks have dirty faces.)

> A young violinist in Rio
> Was seducing a lady named Cleo.
>   As she took down her panties,
>   She said, "No *andantes;*
> I want this *allegro con brio!*"

All the words in the list below are collectively referred to as euphemisms. In the blank write the word each has replaced:

step-ins _____
white meat/dark meat _____, _____
slumber room _____
terminal living _____
extramarital relationship _____
born out of wedlock _____
enceinte _____
derrière _____
water closet (WC) _____

Were you offended when you read the word *panties* in the doggerel above? Would *drawers* have been less indelicate? Or *step-ins*—that's the word that once replaced *drawers,* though why stepping in them is more graceful than drawing them on is far from clear.

Since the dawn of literacy man has had more than a sneaking suspicion that there is some mystical connection between the thing and the word for it. Medieval claptrap? Wilfred Funk says if you doubt this mysticism, then the next time you drive your car, say out loud, "I've never had an automobile accident in all my life"—without wincing or knocking on wood. Give a dog a bad name, and he'll be bad. The reverse of this psychology is often applied; on opening night at the theater an actor never says "Good luck!" to his colleague; he says, "Break a leg!" It's best not to tempt the gods. A Hungarian mother with a new baby is told, "What an ugly child!" for exactly the same reason.

Disagreeable things can somehow be made better by renaming them. Victorian euphemisms (Gk. *eu-,* well + *phanai,* speak) like *white meat/dark meat* for "breast" and "leg" now seem quaint, but they are as common today as they were a century ago. Have you looked recently at the nomenclature for used clothing shops? Whimsical names run from nostalgic flavor ("Second Time Around") to theatrical ("Act Two") to automotive ("Rethreads").

Even the ancient Greeks spoke gently of cemeteries and the dead; a *koimētērion* (sleeping place) bore the same connotation as our modern mortician's *slumber room;* not dead but merely sleeping. Of course it's these latter-day thanatologists who've coined *terminal living* to escape having to say *dying.*

Circumlocution (L. *circum,* around + *loquor,* speak) is absolutely imperative for adultery (now *extramarital relationship*), bastardy (referred to as *born out of wedlock*), and cancer (a *growth*). Half a page of words have been devised for the word *pregnant.*

The apogee of Victorian delicacy came when somebody put stockings on piano legs. The Victorians taught us that anything close to a woman's body must be named with care—that's why women don't wear *shirts;* even *shift* got too strong,* so the French *chemise* was brought in, just as *lingerie* seemed safer than *underthings, enceinte* less biological than *pregnant,* and *derrière* more delicate than *bottom.*

Even at the racetrack (a place never famous for propriety), euphemisms abound: a *whole horse* (stud) is *altered* (castrated) and thus rendered unfit for *servicing* (breeding).

A lexicon could be filled with euphemisms for *toilet.* The word has made a long journey from *toile* (Fr., cloth). Its diminutive, *toilette,* was once a piece of material in which to wrap

---

*When an actor said *shift* in a Dublin play in 1907, the scandalized audience abandoned the theater.

clothes. Later designating a towel or coverlet used by the barber to protect the shoulders of his customer, the word slipped into the boudoir as the linen with which to cover the dressing table, and from there expanded its meaning to include the dressing table and all its appurtenances. Thence the meaning further broadened to encompass all the implements of beauty and the making up itself. With uncharacteristic indelicacy Ivor Brown reminds us in his *Chosen Words* that Pope's "the long labors of the toilet cease" refers to cessation of vanity and not recovery from constipation.

It was in America that *toilet* finally reached the present meaning that has acquired its myriad of renamings. English euphemisms have been summoned for duties here, like *loo, amenities, convenience,* and *WC,* * but here's one stridency the French language cannot assuage: *pissoir* won't do.

Euphemisms will always be with us, for two reasons. The first is that their *raisons d'être* remain unchanged: reverence, modesty, genteelism, and common sense; it's only the vogues that change. Victorians had no more euphemisms for *sex* than the Hebrews had for *God,* and probably fewer than we moderns have for *race*—or *alcoholism, money,* or *class.* In *The State of the Language* Philip Howard traces the circle of *black* replaced by *darky,* then *colored,* then *Negro,* then *Afro-American,* then *non-white,* to—yes, to *black* again. The last example illustrates the second reason: a euphemism quickly takes on the implications of the term it replaced, so that it must be changed periodically. A *servant* became *hired help,* and then *maid,* and now *dayworker;* the *poor* who once looked to *charity* became the

---

*Last summer an Englishman visiting The University of Texas saw the WC (West Campus) shuttle bus and commented, "You Americans put *everything* on wheels!"

underprivileged who relied on *welfare* and now the *disadvantaged* who are aided by the *Department of Human Resources,* while the DHR is already casting about for a "less demeaning" name. The euphemism is alive and well in the twentieth century.

And so is its opposite. The dysphemism* slanders good or neutral things by giving them bad names. Yankee sympathizers with the South were disparagingly called *Copperheads* by those in the North. Nowadays a religious enthusiast might hear his convictions deemed self-serving (when he's called a *Christer*) or even demented (when he's called a *Jesus freak*).

And which side do you think named *scabs,* or *peaceniks,* or *ecofreaks?* Dysphemisms seem destined to be around awhile, too.

Ecdysiasts and *iatronudics* share

> medical origins
> hieratic overtones
> European ancestry
> a desire to disrobe
> a fear of snakes

Ecdysis comes from the science of entomology rather than medicine, describing the process by which insects shed their skins. From it H. L. Mencken coined the humorously pompous *ecdysiast* for "strip-teaser," euphemistic but still a long way from things priestly *(hieratic).*

---

*Nothing new about *dysphemism;* the term is from the nineteenth century.

Women who, under the guise of pretending illness, like to take off their clothes in front of doctors (Gk. *iatros*) are *iatronudics.* A disease brought about by a physician's actions or words, especially an imagined disease, is described as *iatrogenic.*

The most similar item to *pot-au-feu, puchero,* and *bollito misto* is

Irish whiskey
Irish potatoes
Irish stew
"When Irish Eyes Are Smiling"

The prudent practice of boiling up leftover meat and vegetables must be universal, for every culture seems to relish such a dish. Though the French *pot-au-feu* (literally "pot on the fire") seems linguistically a humble meal (the phrase also means "bare existence, bread and butter"), the broth from the cooking, customarily strained and drunk separately, is much rhapsodized by gourmets. Spanish *puchero,* Italian *bollito misto,* and of course Irish stew are variations of the same dish.

A mahout would find most helpful a

keddah
kedge
kedgeree

Not long ago I heard an old friend say something about a mahout he'd seen in a circus. My friend is a knowledgeable but not particularly literary fellow, and I was a little surprised at his answer when I asked if he remembered where he had first heard that word: he looked at me as if I'd been born yesterday and said, "Why, it's out of *The Jungle Book.*" His assumption was that every child had read Kipling, or had had it read to him, and thus remembered the Hindi word for the keeper and driver of an elephant. That same language furnishes the mahout with a useful *keddah* as well, an enclosure for ensnaring wild elephants.

Though a *kedgeree* is an English concoction of fish, rice, and eggs, the dish (and the word) were brought from India, (again Hindi, from the Sanskrit *khicca*).

Kedge has no such exotic meaning or origin. From the earlier English *cadge,* "to warp a ship," a kedge is the light anchor used for that purpose.

The adjectives *morganatic* and *leviratic* describe

    millionaires
    mayors
    marriages
    manufacturers of denim clothing

When Henry VIII proposed to wed Catherine of Aragon, his brother's widow, his supporters quoted precedence and approval from ancient biblical law: Deuteronomy 25:5 not only condoned but required such marriages. But Henry's detractors quoted just the opposite from the same book, for Leviticus

20:21 seems to say that *leviratic* marriage is forbidden and likely to result in childlessness.*

A person of royalty in love with a commoner might be forced by custom or countrymen to propose a *morganatic* union, in which the commoner agrees not to share any titles or estates of the royal or noble partner. The Latin phrase *matrimonium ad morganaticam* literally means "marriage for [no dowry but] the morning gift," i.e., the husband's token gift to his bride on the morning *(morgan)* after the wedding night. Such an arrangement was an option considered by a modern king, Edward VIII, who abdicated the throne to marry (as Duke of Windsor) Wallis Simpson in 1937. No prenuptial agreement was made, English law not recognizing morganatic marriages, and special letters patent denied the new duchess a share in the royal rank.

As a young man Leonardo da Vinci was one of Verrocchio's

protégés
prodigies
progeny

When the Florentine painter Andrea del Verrocchio executed his *Baptism of Christ,* he allowed his young pupil Leonardo to paint in one angel and a bit of landscape. This detail—its superiority recognizable even by the inexperienced eye—revealed that the skill of the teacher had already been surpassed by that of his *protégé,* one whose training and career

---

*Henry's didn't; daughter Mary was queen of England from 1553 to 1558.

are promoted by an influential person. The French word is derived from a Latin term meaning "to protect." And Leonardo was nothing if not a *prodigy,* a person with exceptional talents. Here the Latin root is appropriately the word for "prophetic sign." *Progeny* are one's children or descendants; the artist was not kin to his teacher.

Circle the word that is out of place in the list below:

thrall
maverick
helot
odalisque
chattel

Although "Madam, I am your slave" as a response to an introduction is a bit too much nowadays, "Enthralled" might under some circumstances do very well. The phrases mean the same thing, for a *thrall* is one who is in bondage, a slave. In ancient Sparta the Helot was one of a class of serfs neither slave nor free citizen, but *helot* later described one oppressed by de facto slavery.

The *odalisque* was a popular subject of nineteenth-century painters from Ingres to Manet. From *odalik,* the Turkish word for "chambermaid," the French borrowed this term for a female slave or concubine in a harem; the English adopted the French word intact.

Chattel as a specific word for "slave" grew out of the more generic meaning of the word: "any article of personal, movable property" (from the same medieval Latin *capitale* which later yielded *capital*).

The only word on the list that isn't a synonym for *slave* is of course *maverick.* Texas rancher Samuel Maverick (1803–1870) refused to brand his cattle but set up a loud outcry when his stray animals were not returned to him (because they were not marked). Because of Sam's staunch individualism, the word *maverick* for an unbranded calf expanded to include persons who refuse to abide by the dictates of their group, and later to politicians who won't conform to party lines—free spirits quite the opposite of slaves.

What do these words have in common?

pongee
kowtow
tea
fan-tan
gung ho

It's incongruous that the only language commoner than English has added so few words to our language. The omnivorous acquisitiveness of English and the long history of Oriental immigration to America would suggest the presence of many borrowings, but whether it's the hermetic nature of China or the marked differences in origins, the language of seven hundred million speakers of Mandarin Chinese has accounted for relatively few everyday English words. The prefix *Sino-,* signifying things Chinese, stems from *Ch'in,* the dynastic name of the country and the source of the word *China* itself. *Sinology* is thus the study of China's language and literature; a *sinophile* describes one friendly and receptive to the Chinese, and a *sinophobe* is the opposite.

The soft, thin fabric of Chinese or Indian silk with a knotty weave is *pongee,* from Pekinese Chinese *pen chi* ("made by one's own loom"). A Chinese salutation in which one touches his forehead to the ground to signify respect or submission is called *ko t'ou* ("to bump the head"). The English derivative *kowtow* implies behavior more fawning and obsequious than respectful.

The most popular oriental import is Chinese in name as well as nature. At one time pronounced *tay,* the English word *tea* comes from Mandarin Chinese *ch'a.* Their *pai hao* (white down) is a grade of black tea, *pekoe.* Partial fermentation of the dark leaves before drying produces *oolong* (*wu lung,* black dragon).

The Chinese gambling game called *fan t'an* (repeated division) is one in which a number of counters are placed under a bowl and bets made upon what the remainder will be when they are counted out in fours. A similar game played in the West with cards is *fan-tan.* Here the origin is Cantonese rather than Mandarin Chinese.

Credit may have to be given as much to Pidgin English as to Mandarin Chinese for *gung ho* (Chinese *kung ho,* work together). This slogan of Carlson's Raiders, a World War II Marine detachment, has firmly established itself in English as an adjective meaning "wholehearted, enthusiastically loyal."

Origins of the word *carnival* suggest

revelry
masquerade balls
deprivation
feasting
Ferris wheels

The season just before Lent is called *carnival,* feast days culminating in "fat Tuesday" (Fr. *Mardi gras*), the day in which all the meat in the house is eaten, in order to clear the kitchen for the fasting of Lent. The ultimate Latin roots for *carnival* are *carnis,* "flesh," and *vale,* "farewell." "Farewell, flesh" suggests deprivation rather than feasting or merrymaking.

What do these words have in common?

catcall
mob
cocksure
down in the dumps
dun

Among the numerous descriptions of the word *slang* you can often find "transient." That this adjective does not invariably characterize slang is illustrated by this list of words from Francis Grose's *Dictionary of the Vulgar Tongue,* first published in 1785. Appearing just thirty years after Dr. Johnson's monumental *Dictionary of the English Language,* Grose's work remains not only the first systematic classification of slang but also the primary source for all the writers of this genre thereafter. Remembered as fat and fun-loving (Philip Howard describes him as a sort of linguistic Falstaff), Grose would undoubtedly be delighted if he knew the use to which latter twentieth-century slang has put the homonym of his surname.

Among the 1785 phrases now happily forgotten (e.g., a *gentleman's companion* was slang for a louse), the etymology of *dun* emerges: the eponymous Joe Dun was a Lincoln bailiff who pursued his debt collections so vigorously that his name lost its capitalization and became a verb even in Grose's time.

Nobody uses *gluepot* any more as slang for a minister (who joins men and women together in matrimony), but *cocksure* no longer has so much as a hint of the streets. Once a slang term synonymous with *certain*, "cock-sure" alluded to the cock of a firelock, much more sure to fire than a match.

Though a person in fine fettle nowadays would not describe himself with the *cock-a-whoop* (elevated, in high-spirits, transported with joy) of Grose's age, he might very likely use the eighteenth-century slang *down in the dumps* to convey the feeling of the opposite mood. King Dumpos of Egypt (according to the *Dictionary of the Vulgar Tongue*) died of melancholy, sadly aligning his name forever with low spirits.

Grose detailed to his readers the use of the rude *cat call*, a kind of whistle used by disappointed playgoers "to interrupt the actors, and damn a new piece," writing that its slang name was derived from one of its sounds, "which greatly resembles the modulation of an intriguing boar cat."

Howard's *The State of the Language* says slang has fought uphill battles since earliest times. In a 1711 issue of the *Spectator* Addison disparaged the slang truncation of proper English words: "It is perhaps this Humour of speaking no more than we needs must which has so miserably curtailed some of our Words, as in *mob, rep, pos, incog,* and the like." Though *rep, pos,* and *incog* did indeed prove transient, *mob* is now perfectly acceptable in standard use. Once *mobile vulgus,* the *mobility* was defined by Grose in terms of its opposite, the nobility.* *Mob* is a good example of the slang term that became standard because it filled a hole in the language. Because of its vigor and its heterogeneous origins, slang brings to English a democratic sort of vitality that should be welcomed rather than disparaged.

How are *buccaneers* like *barbeque?*

The French who invaded the Caribbean Islands in the seventeenth century developed a taste for meat the Carib Indians smoked over a wooden rack called a *bocan.* Though *boucaniers* originally meant those who cook their meat in such a fashion, the word (as *buccaneers*) in time came to mean the French pirates themselves.

Such a framework of sticks for roasting meat was called *barbacoa* in American Spanish, the word itself from Haiti. In this case the term for the cooking apparatus was transferred not to the eater but to the food itself: *barbeque.*

---

*Nob hasn't yet made it to standard English; it is still marked *Slang* in modern dictionaries and defined just as in Grose: a man of rank.

What color were these flowers at the time each was given its
name?

carnation
chrysanthemum
crocus
edelweiss
phlox

Since Roman times all carnations have been red, white, or
pink—at least they were until the florist arrived with his dyes.
That the first one ever to be named was pink is suggested by the
Latin root for the term, *carne* (flesh). The Greek "gold flower"
(*chrysos anthemon,* Eng. *chrysanthemum*) offers little doubt as
to its original color, and the same second element sprouts *he-
lianthus, dianthus,* and *anthurium.*

The language of the ancient Greeks was responsible for *crocus*
as well as *phlox,* their titles again indicating their original colors:
krokos is the word for "saffron," while *phlox* means "flame."

Julie Andrews and *The Sound of Music* rescued the *edelweiss*
from Alpine obscurity, and the patriotic tune by that name is
appropriate for the little flower's color and nature (Ger. *edel,*
noble + *weiss,* white).

Match each word with its literal definition:

addled   into the wind
trivial   on the ground
humiliated   without a name
ignominious   like crossroads
aloof   full of urine

Addled is one of the translation errors that enliven the etymology of all languages. The ancient Greek phrase for a spoiled egg was *ourion ōon,* "wind egg," the "wind" ostensibly the hydrogen sulfide gas characteristic of rotten eggs. The translation error probably occurred from similar sounds, for the Roman scribe wrote what he thought he heard: Latin *ovum urinae* ("egg of urine"), in a similarly descriptive vein. Middle English just used their word for urine *(adel)* to describe the spoiled egg, and *addled* soon became synonymous with rotten.

What happened at Roman crossroads (L. *tri-,* three + *via,* road) seemed to have been pretty much what happens at similar places everywhere: people paraded and prattled. What you could hear there didn't amount to much, just *triviālis,* at the crossroads.

From the Latin *humus,* "earth," grew *humilis,* "on the ground," in the sense of "falling on one's face," the figurative position of one disgraced or humbled.

Since civilization's earliest history the power and magic of a name has been noted. From Adam's naming of the animals and his consequent domination of them (i.e., naming a thing gives you power over it) to the Rumplestiltskin Principle (i.e., naming a thing makes it get better), the mystical union of a thing with its name has been indivisible. Nowadays a skillful man acquires "a name for" cookery or boat-building or editing dictionaries. To "have no name" (L. *in-,* not + *nomen,* name) is an *ignominy,* a condition characterized by shame or disgrace.

Dutch seamen who ordered their pilots to steer their ships into the wind to avoid an obstacle have contributed *aloof* (Dutch *a-,* toward + *loef,* luff), and American slang has coined its caveat of "steering away" from an undesirable course of action.

Which would you rather be?

lapidated
lapidous
lapidified
lapped

The Latin word for stone *(lapis)* has spawned an entire page in the OED, but the two derivatives most commonly heard are often misused: your friend who asks you to admire her new *lapis* (when she has acquired jewelry made from lapis lazuli) is speaking in fragments. Similarly wooden houses or (horrors!) people said to be *dilapidated* simply cannot reach that state, however much neglected they are (L. *dis-,* apart + *lapis,* stone).

To be *lapidated* is to be "stoned to death," certainly an undesirable fate, and *lapidous* (full of stones) is little better, a painful if not fatal condition. *Lapidification* is what happened to Lot's wife when she looked back upon the burning cities of Sodom and Gomorrah. Few would seek immortality in such fashion.

To be *lapped* in a footrace—bested by a complete circuit of the track—is an indignity, perhaps even a disgrace, but when compared to the other choices, it's the best by far.

What do these words have in common?

guinea pig
titmouse
ventriloquist
catgut
wormwood

Like Cleopatra's Needle* and Jerusalem artichokes,† these misnomers have enjoyed general use so long that their parentage is no longer suspect. There's nothing porcine about the *guinea pig,* a rodent native to South America. *Titmice* owe nothing to either breasts or rodents; *tit* seems to have been a dialectal word for any small object. No matter how clever he is, a *ventriloquist* can't learn to speak (L. *loqui*) from his stomach (L. *ventri-*). And it was the intestines of sheep, rather than cats, that once provided surgeons and racquet-stringers with *catgut.*

Legend has provided a colorful account of the origin of *wormwood,* the aromatic herb that flavored Hemingway's absinthe. Neither vermiform nor xyloid, the plant is said to have sprung up from the track of Eden's serpent, as he writhed along the ground when driven out of Paradise.

Many well-used phrases can be accurately dated because of their historical origins. In the two lists below match the phrase on the left with the date associated with it on the right.

grinning like a Cheshire cat	1850 B.C.
cross the Rubicon	850 B.C.
between Scylla and Charybdis	49 B.C.
go the whole hog	1640
as numerous as the stars in the sky	1828
People who live in glass houses shouldn't throw stones.	1865

*Erected about 1500 B.C. by Thotmes III.
†Italian *girasole,* "sunflower."

Are overused phrases such as these "hackneyed" because so many of them originated in Hackney? If that's the source, it isn't very appropriate, because the cockneys who come from this London borough freshen their phrases as often as all speakers of slang. The antiquity and color of these phrases vouch for their popularity and to some extent atone for their well-worn edges.

The popular Victorian (1865) author who gave us portmanteau and Humpty-Dumpty words also created the Cheshire Cat, who grinned and grinned as he gradually vanished, until all that was left of him was the grin. Lewis Carroll might be startled to know of the large number of people who use "grinning like a Cheshire Cat" and have not so much as a nodding acquaintance with his *Alice* books.

The writer or speaker who "crosses the Rubicon" convinces his reader or listener that he has taken an irrevocable step. The original phrase was that of an orator no less than Julius Caesar (49 B.C.), who with his army transgressed the boundaries of his province by crossing the Rubicon River into Cisalpin Gaul, thus precipitating war with Italy and Pompey. Classical allusions are to be found wherever you look for them: a popular rock group sings of making "a move across the Rubicon" with ominous and fateful overtones.

Where I live in East Texas, the phrase *between a rock and a hard place* has supplanted *between Scylla and Charybdis,* possibly because the words are difficult to pronounce. Homer's 850 B.C. phrase is no less colorful, and it means the same thing— having to choose between two equally perilous or evil alternatives, neither of which can be avoided without encountering and falling victim to the other. Odysseus' unenviable position was between Scylla, the sea monster who threatened him on one side, and the great whirlpool called Charybdis on the other.

To go the whole hog (spend the entire amount) has to do with swine only numismatically, for the 1828 shilling (and a U.S. dime as well) was coined with a pig stamped on one face. The phrase became popular during Andrew Jackson's presidential campaign that year; he was a "whole-hogger," one who will see the thing through to the bitter end and damn the consequences.

The famous statement "People who live in glass houses shouldn't throw stones" was really "Whose house is of glass, must not throw stones at another," from George Herbert's 1640 *Jacula Prudentum.* Though *Jacula* is nowadays known to few, Herbert's caveat is probably the best-known adage in the list.

Of course the last phrase is the oldest of them all. And it's from what I've always thought is the very best scene in Genesis, where old Abraham, grieving over his childlessness, is summoned from his tent into the inky desert night. The sky above him is luminous with stars, as only total ground darkness can make it, and Yahweh assures the anguished Abraham that his progeny will someday be as numerous as the uncountable stars above him.

Identify this quartet:

Boreas
Notus
Eurus
Zephyrus

From the names of each of the four wind gods has come the term for a different wind. The god in Greek mythology who personified the north wind was *Boreas,* and it is from his name that *boreal* (pertaining to the north) is taken. The ancient overseer of southern winds, *Notus,* generated the *noto-* prefix signifying things southern, like the *Notogaea* (the zoogeographic region including Australia, New Zealand, and the southwestern Pacific Islands) and *notornis,* the flightless bird of New Zealand.

Eurus was god of the east wind, evidently a hot one in his part of the world, for the Greek *heurin,* from which the name *Euros* is derived, means "to singe." That the Ancients found the gentle west wind more salubrious is suggested by their appointment of two gods for it. The Greek *Zephyrus* personifies the west wind; hence *zephyr* has come to mean any gentle breeze, as well as a wind from the west. *Favonius* was the Roman deity, and *favonian* means both "of the west wind" and "benign."

Your friends would find you most lugubrious if they saw you riding

    in a palanquin
    a llama
    a velocipede
    in a charnal cart

The Sanskrit word *paryanka* (bed) has contributed *palanquin,* the East Asian covered litter on poles carried by four bearers. I've always been a little uneasy with the proper pronunciation of pal-an-KEEN, because I first learned it long ago from that catchy old Irish song, "I've Got Rings on My Fingers,

Bells on My Toes," where the composer shoehorned the pronunciation to match his internal rhyme:

> He sat within
> His palanquin. . . .

Ogden Nash is more reliable, providing a whimsical mne-
monic device to differentiate the South American ruminant
from the Buddhist monk:

> The one-l lama he's a priest,
> The two-l llama he's a beast. . . .

If you're like me, you might look ludicrous on a llama—or less
than regal in a palanquin—but not sad.

You probably wouldn't look sad on a *velocipede,* the early
pedal-less bicycle pushed by the rider's feet on the ground (L.
velox, fast + *ped,* feet). Nothing lugubrious here, either.

What your friends would find sad is to see you, or the remains
of you, riding in a *charnel cart* (derived from Latin *carne,* flesh)
to a *charnel house,* "a building or vault to receive the bodies of
the dead."

W hat do these words have in common?

kidvid
Kwok's disease
jargonaut
Jonah word
spork
prefade
wormery

These words all appear in editors Clarence L. Barnhart, Sol Steinmetz, and Robert K. Barnhart's *The Second Barnhart Dictionary of New English,* in which they seek to define neologisms either "not entered or inadequately explained in standard dictionaries."

Like most good neologisms, *kidvid* (*kid,* child + *video,* television) both fills a hole in the language and lends itself to ready interpretation. *Kidvid* illustrates the same affinity for assonance so common in Cockney expressions like *trouble and strife* (wife) and *frog and toad* (road).

Kwok's disease* is an eponym describing the flushing, dizziness, and headache produced by eating food (often Chinese) liberally flavored with monosodium glutamate. The genetic predisposition to the Chinese Restaurant Syndrome is probably less common in Asians than in Westerners—or perhaps the Orientals are just more stoic and seldom report such symptoms.

Jargonaut, a portmanteau word from *jargon* and *argonaut,* describes the person who uses jargon excessively. It's easier to see how *astronaut* is derived from *Argonaut* (one who sailed with Jason on the *Argo* in search of the Golden Fleece) than it is *jargonaut,* and indeed the editors suggest that *argot* has influenced the formation. Journalists have fallen into the annoying habit of displaying their own prejudices by slyly reforming words with pejorative suffixes like *-naut: ecofreak* for "environmentalist," *educationist* for "educator," and *escapenik* for "Russian Jew seeking deportation."

Jonah has had his name associated with jinxes and bad luck since biblical times, when he was tossed overboard to appease

---

*Named for Robert Kwok, the American physician who first described it.

the storm gods. A *Jonah word* is any word with which a chronic
stutterer has difficulty.

Those awful plastic spoons with the blunt tines, like you get
at fast-food restaurants, ought to remain nameless; even the
inelegant *spork* blend is more than they deserve.

Prefade had to be devised for a novel process, to accomodate a
generation of youngsters who prefer their denims to look well-
worn from the start. Before you look askance at such modern-
day perversity, remember the preceding generation's "predirt-
ied" white bucks, in which the makers of white suede shoes
grayed them with dust to meet the fashion demand of the fifties.

Why hasn't *wormery* (formed after the nature of *fishery*)
replaced *worm farm* before now? The inaccurate image of
worms being planted, fertilized, and cultivated surely has suffered an overdue demise. Does this mean that *horsery* will soon
supplant *horse farm?* The editors of *The Second Barnhart Dictionary* do not speculate.

Match each exclamation from the list on the left with its
meaning from the list on the right.

Eureka!	before our patron saint
Zounds!	like a maggot
Zany!	the cart before the horse
Mawkish!	John
Preposterous!	God's wounds
By George!	I have found (it).

Eureka! is possibly the world's oldest popular interjection,
for it was more than two millennia before our time that Hiero,

ancient king of Syracuse, asked his favorite mathematician to devise a way to calculate the percentage of gold in the royal crown. At first unable to come up with a method of doing so, Archimedes filed the problem away in his mind and went on to other duties. Then—in the manner of many historic inspirations—the answer to the problem came to him at a time when he was distracted by more mundane thoughts. Lowering himself into his bath and watching the consequent water level change in the tub, he suddenly shouted his famous *"Eureka!"* (Gk. *heurēka,* I have found [it]). He reasoned that he might measure water displacement of the crown and compare it with separate displacements of known weights of gold and silver, thus establishing the fractions of each metal making up the crown.

In Shakespeare's *King John* the character Philip the Bastard, a half-brother to Faulconbridge, exclaims ruefully and impiously:

> Zounds! I was never so bethump'd with words
> Since I first call'd my brother's father dad.

After the manner of *gosh!* (God) and *gee!* (Jesus) and *heck!* (hell), *zounds!*—variously spelled *zwounds, s'wounds,* and *z'wounds,* depending on the period—is a euphemism for "God's wounds."

At one time Venetian dialect substituted *Zanni* for the regular Italian *Gianni,* itself a diminutive of *Giovanni* (John). A comedian by that name who played the part of a servant in the Italian theater became so popular that *zani* got to be the word for any servant. By the time the word made it to England, the character's comedy was evidently remembered better than his class, so that *zany* is now synonymous with "ludicrous." Just as in the slang for *toilet,* it's all rather pejorative for poor old John.

Modern usage restricts *mawkish* pretty much to "excessively and objectionably sentimental," but the earlier sense of the adjective (nauseating) stemmed from Middle English *mathek* (maggot), certainly an appropriate figure for this unpleasant sight.

An absurdity like *the chicken before the egg* suggests a situation at variance with the laws of nature, unnatural. One Latin word itself demonstrates such a contrary state of affairs: *praeposterus* (from *prae,* before + *posterus,* coming after).

Officially the patron saint of England since the Order of the Garter (c. 1348), St. George had been invoked by British soldiers who cried "Before George!"* as early as the Crusades at Antioch (1089). Though George was undoubtedly a historical character, the apocryphal tale of his slaughtering the dragon (at a pond near Silene, Libya) is more in keeping with the flavor of the modern interjection.

T̲he name of a conquering hero is most likely to be found in an

  acalculia
  academy
  accolade
  Aceldama
  acrology

---

*Some years before exclaiming "By George!"

So many of us are afflicted with *acalculia* (ă-kăl-KŪ-lĭ-ə, from L. *a-,* unable + *calculāre,* to calculate) that the word for this condition ought to be better known than it is. A disinclination to work with numbers must be fairly common among those who enjoy etymology.

Greek mythology has it that a Spartan farmer called Akademos once helped Castor and Pollux (who now are literally stars) locate their kidnapped sister Helen. The grateful brothers rewarded the farmer handsomely for his assistance: the grove of Akademos was eternally watched over by the gods. When Plato chose this favored spot for his dialogues and lectures, the place was called in Greek *Akadēmia,* and *academy* became the English word for a place of learning.

Aceldama might be the least likely spot for a conquering hero. Named from the Aramic *haqel demā* (field of blood), this potter's field near Jerusalem reputedly was bought with the reward money Judas received for betraying Jesus. Judas returned the money to the priests, who used it to purchase burial ground for paupers and strangers. So unpleasant are its connotations that an Aceldama can be any place with dreadful associations.

The science of using initials, pictures, or symbols to represent names is called *acrology* (Gk. *akros*, extremity + *logos,* word). This consumer world of ours is replete with rebuses, from the universal symbols on the controls of Japanese automobiles to the signs on the doors of public restrooms—sometimes to the point of a sort of linguistic reductionism that makes you a little uneasy.

In times past a conquering hero might be knighted in a ceremony climaxed by a tap on the neck (L. *collum*) with the flat of a sword. In addition to its connotations of praise and approval, an *accolade* can be an embrace (from Provençal *acolada*) or simply a hug around the neck (L. *ad-*, to + *col-lum*).

Infanticipating, absobloominlutely, and *guarandamntee* are examples of a word formation called

aposiopesis
elision
tmesis
schizophraxia

When I was a child the commonest *aposiopesis* on the radio—the first in my memory—was Fibber McGee's "I'll just look here in the hall closet, and—." Nobody was surprised and everybody was delighted with the subsequent long sound track of articles falling from the overloaded closet shelves. The Greek *aposiōpēsis* (a becoming silent) is a sudden and dramatic breaking off of a thought in the middle of a sentence, as though the speaker were unwilling (or unable, as in the case of Fibber McGee) to continue. Try out your ear and you'll hear that everyday spoken English is filled with aposiopeses.

As well as with *elisions* (the omitting of a vowel or syllable in speech). In East Texas informal speech "probly" is so common that a speaker who pronounces "probably" might be thought to be putting on airs. I asked a hundred college freshmen to listen carefully during the entire twenty-eight days of February to try to hear anybody pronounce something other than "Febuary," and the only place they heard it pronounced intact was from diction-trained television news reporters.

A *tmesis* (Gk., a cutting) comes close to the answer: "the separation of the parts of a compound word by one or more

intervening words." When Eliza Doolittle sings, "Oh, so lov-
erly, sitting *absobloominlutely* still," and Archie Bunker
growls, "Yankees win the pennant? I *guarandamntee* you they
will!," their figures of speech qualify as tmeses. But Walter
Winchell's "The John LaGattas are *infanticipating*" fails to
enclose any word completely and is thus simply a blend. Only
the more inclusive *schizophraxia* will answer for all three (Gk.
schizo-, split + *phrasis*, speech).

W̲hat do these words have in common?

aquiline
uncate
aduncous
hamulate
unguiform

Why is it that some words have pages of synonyms (like
famous and *toilet*) and others are so exclusive that they must
be borrowed from another tongue (like *schadenfreude* from
German and the French borrowing *le weekend*)? You can theo-
rize that *famous* became overworked enough to need fresh
alternatives, and that *toilet* requires synonyms for propriety's
sake, but what about the meaning "hook-shaped"? Nothing is
improper or delicate here, and it's far from overworked. Yet
aquiline (hooked like an eagle's beak); *uncate, uncinate,* and
unguiform (L. *uncus,* hook); and *hamulate* (L. *hamus,* hook)
all describe the same humble shape. Such profusion is one of the
reasons that English is more complex—as well as larger in
vocabulary—than other languages.

Draw these words:

breve _____
recipe _____
asterisk _____
carat _____
caret _____

The *breve* is the symbol (˘) above a vowel showing that it has a short (L. *brevis,* brief) sound. Remember păt/pĕt/pĭt/pŏt/pŭtt, and you'll never have to look at another dictionary key for the sound of a breve.

Medical students are blithely taught that the symbol ℞ means "take thou," the implication being that the patient would know to take (L. *recipere*) the prescription that followed. Actually the early physicians' instructions were to the apothecary rather than the patient, and his *recipe* said to "take this and mix it with that . . ." Since drugs are no longer compounded by pharmacists, the notion of a recipe hasn't much meaning nowadays.

An *asterisk* (*) is a little star (Gk. *asteriskos*), just as the daisy-like *aster* looks like a star (Gk. *astēr*), but planetoids evidently bear less resemblance and so are only *asteroids.*

The origin of a *carat* (*c.* 200 mg, as a unit of weight for precious metal or gems) depends upon which history you read. The scales' counterweight pan might have contained little bits of horn (Gk. *keration*) or evergreen seeds (Old French *carobs*) of known weight.

To splice an overlooked word into a sentence, an editor points to a superscript with a *caret* (∧), signifying "there is lacking," from Latin *carēre,* "to be without."

When Antony says to Cleopatra, "Let's have one other *gaudy* night," he has on his mind

an orgy
sexual adventure
a fancy dress ball
a big meal
drunken oblivion

The Elizabethans got a lot more mileage out of *gaudy* than we do now. When Polonius advised his son Laertes in his famous "To thine ownself be true" speech from *Hamlet,*

> Costly thy habit as thy purse can buy,
> But not expressed in fancy; rich, not gaudy;

he used the word in our modern sense of "tastelessly fine," but Antony invoked the same word in its role of "feast":

> Come,
> Let's have one other gaudy night: call to me
> All my sad captains; fill our bowls once more;
> Let's mock the midnight bell.

The only survivor of the word in this sense seems to be the British *gaudy,* an annual university dinner, often with the flavor of a reunion.

The faithful of the sixteenth century counted their prayers on yet another *gaudy,* the large bead on a rosary separating the decades of smaller *ave* beads. It was this final sense that eventually brought us *gaud* for "bauble, toy, plaything."

P*hilip, chivalrous,* and *recalcitrant* all suggest

dogs
cats
horses
cows
sheep

The archetypal Greek *Philippos* (*philo-,* lover + *hippos,* horse) could have been a racing buff who spent his afternoons at the *hippodrome* (Gk. *dromos,* racecourse). From the imaginations of his fellows sprang the *hippogriff,* half horse and half griffin, and the *hippocampus,* half horse and half fish.

Two Latin words for horse, *equus* and *caballus,* begat a host of English words. From the former comes *equestrian* (of or pertaining to horsemanship) and *equerry* (one who supervises the king's stables). *Caballus* through its derivative *caballārius,* "horseman," yielded *chevalier* and *cavalier,* gentlemen accomplished in arms, and their knightly brand of manners, *chivalry.*

Recalcitrant gets its equine image from the peculiar way a balky horse kicks: back (L. *re-*) + with the heel (L. *calx*).

A *shamus,* a *fly ball,* and a *hawkshaw* are all

money merchants
birds of prey
street vendors
detectives
insects

From the Aramaic *shəmmash,* "to serve," and the cognate Hebrew *shāmmāsh,* "a sexton or beadle in a synagogue," a *shamus* has somehow through modern peregrinations come to be a private detective, perhaps because a Jewish shammes has more to do with keeping order in his synagogue than does a sexton in a church.

Since a *fly* in American slang is "an alert, knowing person," and *to be fly* is to be nimble-minded, *fly ball* as a name for a detective seems to be complimentary rather than disparaging. Frequently hyphenated, *fly ball, fly cop, fly dick, fly mug,* and *fly bob* are other forms, the last with a nod to Sir Robert Peel, 1828 organizer of London's police force and eponymous donor to the language of *bobby, peeler,* and *Robert,* all nicknames for police officials of one rank or another.

Hawkshaw was the detective's name in Tom Taylor's 1863 *The Ticket-of-Leave-Man.* * In the manner of George du Maurier's *Trilby (svengali)* and Rabelais' *Gargantua and Pantagruel (gargantua),* the character has outlived the vehicle that introduced him, lost his capitalization, and become a useful English word.

Though each of these women was famous in her own time, each was later remembered for what else?

Amelia Jenks Bloomer
Maria Lee
Lucy Stone
Bertha Krupp
Dame Nellie Melba

---

*And also the gumshoe in Gene Mager's comic strip, "Hawkshaw the Detective."

By the time Mrs. Bloomer designed the garment that made her name famous, she had already distinguished herself in the cause of women's rights. Editor and publisher of *The Lily,* a temperance magazine and the first magazine in America to be edited by a woman, she fell in with the new U.S. Women's Rights Movement. In 1850 she hosted a New York benefit ball in which she specified the appropriate dress:

> We would have a skirt reaching down to nearly halfway between the knee and the ankle, and not made quite so full as is the present fashion. Underneath the skirt, trousers moderately full, in fair mild weather, coming down to the ankle (not instep) and there gathered in by an elastic band . . . For winter, or wet weather, the trousers also full, but coming down into a boot, which should rise some three or four inches at least above the ankle.

Though the subsequent "Bloomer girls" were not considered unfashionable, the garment was much ridiculed, possibly laying the connotative foundation for its present-day implications, for now the eponym *bloomers* is a jocular term for women's underwear.

Maria Lee was a black woman of amazonian strength and proportion who operated a shabby Boston resident hotel. Not only did she often blow the whistle on her drunken and criminal customers, she actually helped the police with their arrests. Perhaps because linguistic bullying of the Irish was unpopular in Boston, the name for the paddy wagon used to haul crooks to jail was changed to *Black Maria.*

It's a little surprising that *Lucy Stoner* seems to be falling into obscurity, for a new bride's practice of retaining her own name, rather than taking her husband's, seems to be ever more common. The nineteenth-century suffragist Lucy Stone refused to relinquish her surname when she married a Mr. Blackwell.

Like Mae West, Bertha Krupp seems to have immortalized her name not through her deeds but by her stature. Heiress to the mighty German armament empire, Bertha Krupp von Bohlen und Halbach evidently resembled the short, fat silhouette of the World War I howitzers that shelled France, the *Big Berthas*.

Helen Mitchell Armstrong was an Australian coloratura soprano who sang her way to fame as Gilda in *Rigoletto*. Soon made prima donna of the Royal Opera at Covent Garden, London, she became the darling of Englishmen from Shaw (who rhapsodized upon her voice) to George V (who made her Dame of the British Empire in 1918). She took the stage name *Melba* from Melbourne, near her birthplace.

Planning a party with the Ritz's famous chef, George Auguste Escoffier, Dame Nellie Melba opted for *pêches flambées* but found Escoffier in favor of an ice. The chef compromised by amalgamating the two desserts and topping them with whipped cream: *pêches Melba.* *

How is

enthusiastic like *giddy*?
a *kangaroo* like a *nitwit*?
a *vasistas* like a *transom*?

The Britisher who nicknamed the carousel *giddy-go-round* was like me in at least one way, because the things always made me dizzy. But the Old English word *gydig* meant "god-pos-

---

*Lady Melba's Australian countrymen immortalized another famous stage personality with a dessert consisting of a meringue shell filled with tropical fruit and covered in cream, the *pavlova*.

sessed," as does the Greek *enthousiastēs* (*en,* in the power of + *theos,* god).

It might come as a pleasant surprise to many Americans to discover that they already know a sentence in the language of the Australian aborigine. Nowadays everybody knows what a *kangaroo* is, but this was not always true. In 1770 Captain Cook arrived in Australia and was doing his best with the new language when a specimen of that marsupial hopped by. The captain asked the name of the curious animal, and a native replied, "I don't know," in his own tongue. To Cook's ears the sentence sounded like *kangaroo,* and the European name for this beast was thus fixed forever.

And *nitwit* ought to mean "having the wit of a nit (a young louse)"; indeed, a good many dictionaries suggest that this is so. But *niet wit* is the way the Dutch say "I don't know."

How on earth did the French word for "transom" turn out to be *vasistas,* the German sentence for "What is that?" *(Was ist das)*?

Kangaroo, niet wit. You can make up your own story for it.

Index

A page number in **boldface** type indicates the main discussion of the term.